The GIFT of LOVE

Jeffrey David Ringold

To order additional copies of The Gift of Love, or to view upcoming events, please visit us online:

The Human Fulfillment Institute
www.humanfulfillment.org

For online support tools that complement the practices included in this book, please visit Renewal Space:
www.renewalspace.net

The author wishes to offer heartfelt thanks to Paul Wagner and Colleen O'Driscoll for their wise, incisive editorial comments on an early draft of The Gift of Love.

ISBN: 145386444X
ISBN-13: 9781453864449

Praise for Jeffrey David Ringold's previous work, *Living Joy*:

"A powerful guide for anyone who wants their life to be an expression of the awakened heart and mind. Jeffrey Ringold clearly articulates perennial wisdom teachings, and makes them refreshingly applicable to our contemporary lives. Through engaging personal stories, inspirational poetry, and accessible meditations, the reader is offered the radical invitation to realize and inhabit the very essence of what we are."

Tara Brach, author of Radical Acceptance

When I first read Living Joy, I found it full of insights and stories that woke me up and gave me one "aha" after another. The second time I read it, the same thing happened. How do I live a more loving life — not just a bunch of bumper sticker wisdom, but how do I really, actually live it? This book is a good coach.

Frank Andrews, PhD, author of The Art and Practice of Loving.

"I'm not usually a big fan of spiritual and personal growth literature, but this one's in a completely different category. Ringold's writing is extraordinarily deep, lucid, even luminous."

Joseph Esposito, The Portable CEO, Former President, Merriam Webster and CEO, Encyclopedia Britannica

As a training and supervising psychoanalyst with decades of clinical experience and a commitment to integrating mindfulness practice into my psychoanalytic practice, I find this book a wonderful offering. Ringold's book is one I will gladly offer to my own patients and to my supervisees to help them and their own patients aim their lives away from suffering and toward joy. I personally would rate this book five stars.

Harriet Kimble Wrye, Ph.D., ABPP, FIPA

Living Joy is filled with many practical examples of how imperfect, busy people can improve their relationships with themselves, their loved ones, and the imperfect world within which they live — not from within monastery walls, but in the real world, where the rubber hits the road.

Carolyn Blackman, RN LCSW

Wow! Living Joy is a brilliant blend of art and science. Ringold uses the experiences of the human community to teach us and to invite us into our own experience. He makes it safe and okay for us to be where we are. He also invites us into expanding our experience through the use of his new techniques to make the learning real for us.

Deborah J Doig, Life and Executive Coach

I loved this book. Living Joy is a delightful, powerful, and very compelling read. It's as fun to read as it is thought provoking - packed with realistic examples and no-nonsense calls to action.

Andrew Sheridan, Life and Executive Coach and Entrepreneur

Excellent book – a comfortable, easy read, felt like the author was in the room with me, telling anecdotes to guide me. Ringold is a wonderful storyteller, and he weaves his own experiences and others' stories into the teaching. For retreat/workshop leaders, coaches, and trainers: Ringold shares some useful exercises that could be done in trainings or with clients. Illuminating!

Dawn Harry, Life Coach and Workshop Leader

Table of Contents

"Freedom"

from the Gothic "frijon"

and Old English "friga:"

"to love"

Introduction

Pick up a book called "*The Gift of Love*," and you might expect to find a warm, fuzzy quilt of quaint sayings and sentimental poetry. This is not that book. This one's more like a bonfire. It's designed to help you burn away whatever isn't true, deep and alive in your life.

The standard message in most books is that you have to love yourself before you can love anyone else. Here we take the exact opposite approach. By rooting yourself in love of others, you open the door to self-acceptance and a powerful source of inner freedom. When you then turn to loving yourself, you get to explore what that really means as a practical skill instead of just an abstract idea. By learning to care less *about* yourself, and care more *for* yourself, you can discover a powerful key to happiness that very few people ever discover.

That isn't to say that happiness is necessarily the ultimate goal here. Happiness may be more like a byproduct of love than its goal. It all depends what you mean by happiness and what you mean by love. For some of us, there may be times when we think another cigarette, a shot of bourbon, or a moment of revenge will make us happy. You might say that you "love" ice cream or football or romantic comedies. But those aren't quite the things we're talking about here.

What does it mean to truly love yourself or another? What does it mean to love life itself? Get real about those questions and they can quickly turn your own life upside down. Love connects you to what's most uniquely "you," and it also connects you to something universal, to a stream of life that's much larger than your own personal story. If you really give yourself to that larger stream, there's no telling where it will take you. But you'll be lucky to ride its currents wherever they may lead. For though it can never be owned, love remains the single greatest gift that life has to offer. Please enjoy it and pass it along.

Chapter One:
Rooting In Love

A Message from the Planet Zeptone

When I was a kid growing up in New England, I used to walk to school in the snow about a half-mile or so each day during the winter. As I was walking, I'd sometimes imagine that there were strange, beneficent "light beings" up in the sky, keeping me company on my way. Occasionally, I'd get into conversations with these sky-dwellers, and during one conversation, they explained to me that I had been sent from their planet to do something special to help people on earth.

With the inquisitive mind of a first grader, I naturally had to know the name of my home planet. And so, upon asking, I was informed that I hailed from the planet Zeptone – a distant sphere which scientists had yet to discover but which was, nevertheless, an important source of intergalactic gallantry.

One of the kindest acts I ever remember my mother undertaking came when I told her about my secret origins. After asking if could tell her something that sounded crazy, she managed to keep a perfectly straight face the entire time as I explained to her that despite appearances, I in fact came from the planet Zeptone. A year or so later, she asked me whether I still believed I came from another planet. I told her I didn't think so any more, and without so much as a grin, she said "okay, I just wanted to know."

We're Made for More

Kids can be crazy like that, but sometimes in their own strange way, they know something that adults have a way of forgetting.

However much the daily grind may come to dominate our lives, many of us have a sense that there's something more here than meets the eye. There's something beyond the roles we play from day-to-day, something more than our to-do lists — something bigger than all that. We may suspect that we're actually different than we seem, or more than we've become.

If nothing else, maybe we just know that we're made for more than worrying and complaining about our lot or the state of the world. The great playwright George Bernard Shaw once said:

"This is the true joy in life, being used for a purpose recognized by yourself as a mighty one. Being a force of nature instead of a feverish, selfish little clod of ailments and grievances, complaining that the world will not devote itself to making you happy."

Getting in touch with this spirit even a bit can have a major effect on our lives. We don't need to fulfill some great intergalactic mission or destiny. We just need to remember what matters most to us, to see for ourselves what leads to a life of real joy, depth, and fulfillment.

An Imaginary Line

Here's a way of looking at our basic choice. Imagine for a moment that there's a sharp dividing line that runs through the center of life. On one side of the line, there's tremendous misery and unnecessary suffering. On the other side, there's great joy, and a deep appreciation for life's essential beauty.

For the purposes of our exploration, we'll call the first side the World of *Ego*. And we'll call the second side the World of *Love*.

Of course, psychologists, philosophers, poets and ordinary folks use words like love and ego in many different ways. And we know the world isn't *really* divided neatly down the middle. But we can use the terms ego and love in this way to help us paint a clear picture of two very different approaches to life.

Ego and Love

In the World of Ego, you're constantly protecting, defending and competing. You're always looking over your shoulder to see how you measure up. You worry about money and security, and you chase after whatever you think will make you happy. But nothing ever really does. As soon as you get one carrot, there's another one to chase after. Something always seems to be missing or just out of reach, so you never really come to rest.

In the World of Love, life is a gift. You find cause for joy in the simplest of things: the sky, the sun, a child's laughter. Although your circumstances are sometimes pleasant and sometimes challenging, love brings an abiding sense of acceptance and resilience amidst the changes.

The more that love becomes a way of life instead of a feeling that comes and goes, the more it can provide a stable source of well-being that doesn't depend on specific conditions. Love connects you to other people, and it can also connect you to something more enduring, so that whatever twists or turns your own personal journey takes, a part of you can always feel at home and at peace.

Just what all this means and how it functions is a topic that we'll explore over the coming pages. But first, we need a bit more clarity about this distinction between love and ego.

The Habit of Separation

What we mean here by ego is basically just your idea of yourself, your self-image – and the corresponding feeling in your gut that you're separate. This is slightly different from what some psychologists mean when they use the term, and it's also different from what people commonly think of when they say things like "he's got a big ego."

As we use the term, "ego" isn't necessarily some immoral, arrogant thing; it's just a bit misguided. It's a habit of thinking and feeling that you exist as a separate, self-contained "me." But that one little innocent mistake can cause a whole heap of trouble.

What we mean by love... well, that's what we're about to explore.

The Consolation Prize

One of my favorite statements on love, and how it differs from the motivations of the ego, was written by Nobel Prize-winning biologist George Wald. It's a letter he wrote in response to a woman who complained about an idea that was floating around at the time to start a sperm bank for Nobel laureates. The woman found the idea sexist, and asked "why not an egg bank?" So Wald replied:

"You're right, Pauline. It takes an egg as well as a sperm to start a Nobel laureate. Every one of them has had a mother as well as a father. Say all you want of fathers, their contribution to conception is really rather small.

But think of a man so vain as to insist on getting a superior egg from an egg bank. Then he has to fertilize it. And when it's fertilized, where does he go with it, to his wife? "Here, dear," you can hear him saying, "I just got this superior egg from an egg bank and just fertilized it myself. Will you take care of it?" "I've got eggs of my own to worry about," she replies. "You know what you can do with your superior egg. Go rent a womb, and while you're at it, you better rent a room too."

You see, it just won't work. For the truth is that what one really needs is not Nobel laureates but love. How do you think one gets to be a Nobel laureate? Wanting love, that's how. Wanting it so bad one works all the time and ends up a Nobel laureate. It's a consolation prize."

Human Motivation

What an amazing statement: *the Nobel Prize is a consolation prize.* If you look closely, it's not hard to see what Wald is pointing to. A huge portion of what we human beings do is usually tied in one way or another to our desire for love. Other than basic survival, it is perhaps the main human motivation.

Of course, we can act tough and pretend that we don't need anyone's love. But that's just a false pretense of strength that only serves to undermine our capacity for *true* strength. Think for example of a tree's branches getting blown around in a storm. Which branches are the strongest? The tough grey ones? Or the soft green ones? The healthiest branches are supple and alive, because they offer and receive nourishment from the tree, the sunlight, and everything that surrounds them.

In the same way, if you want to be strong, you first have to recognize that your strength comes from your connection to others and to life itself. Separate and on your own, you're bupkus — you're literally nothing at all. Being honest, sensitive, open to other people and to the world, you find your real source of strength. No one is an island. We *all* need love.

Or do we? Let's look closer.

The Big Shift

It's not hard to see how much of human motivation is, either overtly or covertly, a desire for love. Beneath the surface, that's what a lot of the desire for other things like wealth and status and even pleasure are often about. The problem, of course, is that seeking love the way we usually do doesn't work very well. Because life's circumstances are so fickle and fleeting, our hunger for love, success, respect, accomplishment, security, pleasure, and pretty much everything else we can point to is rarely satisfied for very long.

So, here's where the big shift comes in. What if we reverse the process? What if we focus on giving love instead of getting it? That may seem ridiculously simple, nauseatingly sweet, moralistic or just plain dull — but that's only if you don't actually check it out for yourself. If you do check it out, if you get really focused about it, you may discover that this one simple shift can have surprisingly transformative effects on virtually every aspect of your life.

Take relationships for example. When your focus is firmly on loving, though you may still have a "need" for human connection and support, you quickly become a whole lot less "needy." In fact, paradoxically, if you truly love someone, there's a sense in which you don't need them at all. You don't need them because you aren't bargaining for anything in return. Yes, your love connects you, but it also frees you from a sense of dependence.

And that's just one small taste of the freedom that love confers.

Love and Let the Cards Fall as They Will

So here's the basic practice: you act with love as your motivation, and let the cards fall as they will. If you're adored and get a hero's welcome, great. If you're made a fool of, so be it. Love knows no shame; it needs nothing and no one to affirm it.

Whatever the endeavor, you do your best, but you detach your sense of well-being from the outcome, and place it squarely on your intention to act with love. If you ask someone out on a date, your core focus is on expressing love, not on getting anything. If you give a presentation for work, or speak in public, your primary focus is on honestly expressing yourself and acting in service to others, not on looking a particular way. If you confront a serious challenge with your health, finances, or personal life, you do your best to contend with the situation, but you rest in the knowledge that love is your essential source of freedom and well being — regardless of how the circumstances unfold.

Do you feel the gravity of that? It's not some trite Pollyanna acceptance or optimism. It's a very sober choice about where you place your focus. Though your love is likely to benefit others, it frees *you* before it does anything for anyone else. The act of loving has a profoundly healing effect. It fills the longing, aching feeling in the chest that we feel when we go *seeking* for love. It calms anger and anxiety, and melts the sense of separation that's at the root of so much suffering.

Intention is the Core

To say it another way, love brings a healthy kind of self-reliance. To the degree that you're really rooted in love, whatever the world judges a success or failure is none of your concern. Though you do your best to be outwardly effective, the only standard by which you check yourself, the "true north" of your heart's compass, is the purity of your own intention.

It's not that you're a saint, that your intention is always perfect, or even that you adhere to some lofty moral code. It's just that you know how totally unreliable the fortunes of the world are. Loss, gain, pleasure, pain, fame and shame are all the same. They're all equally fickle.

As you root yourself more and more in your own loving intention, there's a way that your heart naturally comes to rest. Perhaps you already know this experience, or perhaps it seems like a stretch. Either way, as long as you don't succumb to too much cynicism or self-judgment, the sense of it can grow stronger and more palpable as you go along.

Trusting in Love

Love's ability to provide solace amidst life's changes makes it radically different from most other sources of fulfillment. Really, how many foundations of happiness can any of us point to that are truly lasting and reliable? Go through the list: Your job? Your friends? Your family? The roof over your head? Your body? What, if anything, can you truly count on?

If you're honest, the answer is: almost nothing. Whatever the world gives you, it can take away. In the blink of an eye, life can take your possessions, your status, your health, or even the people you care about.

But there's one thing that life can't take away. It can't take away your ability to choose love. That's always in your power, and no one can ever confiscate it. There's no way to reliably control all of life's circumstances, but you always have a choice about how you respond. Whatever the situation, you always have some opportunity to shine, however faint or hidden the possibility may seem at the time.

Foolish Wagers

So where will you put your chips?

On the fluctuations of your bank account? On how other people respond or what they think about you? On that body of yours that's growing older even as you read these words, and that will be gone before you know it?

People like to play the odds: "I'll probably live to be seventy-eight, I'll probably have such and such a balance in my bank account, I'll probably find happiness through path A or path B."

But the odds don't matter. Either something is reliable or it isn't. If you're calculating your path to happiness, if you're frantically trying to control the circumstances of life to have it all turn out just right, or even if you're just overly preoccupied with how other people see you, you're caught on a treadmill. You're chasing after a security that can never be found. If you want security in circumstances, you have to get born somewhere else. Here on earth, it's not to be found. (It's the same on Zeptone, I'm told.)

Calling Off the Chase

To be clear, none of this means that there's anything wrong with wanting health, financial security, romance, or whatever else you may want to see come into your life. The seductiveness of the treadmill, though, is that we can get convinced that whatever we're chasing after will actually bring us lasting happiness. If only we can get the carrot, *then* we can finally come to rest. The problem is that there's always another carrot that shows up with the same promise. It may seem like the stress and tension in our lives comes from what we don't have or what we'd like to get rid of. But much of it actually comes from the chase itself. Chasing actually *fuels* our craving for whatever it is we're chasing after.

So whatever you may find yourself chasing after in your life, whatever you imagine will bring future happiness, what would it be like to just call off the chase? I don't mean that you should quit your job or abandon your family and friends. Nor do I mean that you can't take action to improve your circumstances. I just mean that you can allow yourself the liberty of finally coming to rest. You can allow for the possibility that you and your life are actually okay just as you are, even though things may be difficult at times.

When you do then take action, you can actually be much more effective, because your actions are guided by freedom rather than compulsion. Your actions take on a kind of ease and spontaneity, because you aren't trying to control a million outcomes that can never really be controlled. You just love, and let action flow as it will.

Love Is An Ability

This sense of "flow" is actually very important. Although we talk about "choosing" love, it's often less a choice than a force that naturally expresses itself when we aren't "ego-ing" ourselves into separation. When we aren't worrying, obsessing, concocting stories in our heads, or thinking ourselves into a separate sense of self, we're naturally open and receptive. Then love has a way of flowing through us effortlessly, just like water flows through a clear, open channel.

At other times, love truly is a conscious, committed choice that emerges from the very core of the human spirit. If you've ever seen or heard one of those exceptional people who has been experienced terrible cruelty and violence, and has chosen reconciliation rather than hatred, then you know what I'm talking about. The ability of such people to love comes only on the heels of a supremely courageous, resolute choice. It's not just flow, but also fire. Martin Luther King Jr. comes to mind:

Have we not come to such an impasse in the modern world that we must love our enemies - or else? The chain reaction of evil - hate begetting hate, wars producing more wars - must be broken, or else we shall be plunged into the dark abyss of annihilation.

So, openness to love may sometimes seem willful and it may sometimes seem like a spontaneous movement of "grace." In either case, it's usually most helpful to see it as a matter of *receptivity* rather than passivity, and *willingness* rather than willfulness.

But it's still bigger than that. Love isn't *only* a feeling, a choice, or an expression of grace, but also a kind of *ability*. It's something that moves in the world spontaneously, *and* it's something that can absolutely be practiced and learned on deeper and deeper levels. Like most abilities, whether we're talking about golfing, cooking, or playing the cello, the more that love is consciously practiced and renewed, the more it becomes a kind of "second nature" that functions on its own.

So let's turn now to the actual practice of love and see what we discover.

Chapter Two:
Practices Of Love

Showing Up for Love

Let's see if we can challenge ourselves a bit. There are probably people in our lives whom we love dearly, but the hard question is: *do we really love the people we love?* In other words, do we act in ways that genuinely express the best that our hearts have to offer?

Love can mean a lot of different things and can take many forms. But this much is clear: It's one thing to feel love; it's another to actually express it with any kind of consistency. How, in the most practical sense, can we cultivate the ability to express love more fully?

As simple as it may sound, the first and foremost requirement of practicing love is that we have to actually make it our central focus and priority. If we're constantly distracted, worrying and chasing after external sources of fulfillment, it's easy for people to end up playing second fiddle. Our to-do list becomes the master of our lives, and the more we rush to complete it, the more we become its slave. The following story shows just how powerful the process can be.

A Matter of Time

Princeton University researchers John Darley and Daniel Batson once conducted an experiment that tested people's ability to act with empathy. They required a group of seminary school students to present a lecture to a large audience in a nearby building. One group was instructed to lecture about seminary jobs, the other about the biblical story of the Good Samaritan, who helped a wounded man along the road to Jericho.

The group was also divided into those who answered in a questionnaire that they saw their religious studies mainly as a personal religious quest, and those who saw it primarily as a means of compassionate service. Finally, a third of the group was told they had plenty of time before presenting their lecture, a third was told they had only a little time, and a third was told they were late and had to rush.

As part of the experiment, on the way to the lecture hall, the students all encountered a man who was slumped over, apparently injured, moaning in great pain. Some of the students stopped to help the man. Some indirectly helped by asking for assistance when they got to the hall. And a number of students totally disregarded the man's pleas for help, stepping over his grieving body and ignoring his plight in order to get to the lecture hall so they could give their talk.

Here's what the study found. Neither the reason for the student's religious study, nor the assigned lecture subject had any significant effect on who provided help. Whether they saw their studies primarily as a personal quest or as a means to help others made little difference. Even if they were about to give a lecture on the story of the Good Samaritan, it had no significant effect on the likelihood of the students taking time to help the man. The *only* significant factor that influenced whether or not the students provided help was whether or not they were in a hurry.

What does this tell us about living a loving life – not in theory but in actual practice? Does it say anything about the focus of your own life? Is there anything that you find yourself chasing after, and anything that you miss when you're caught in the chase?

Which Seeds Will You Water?

A second practical element that affects our ability to love is also about mental and emotional focus, but it's a different kind of focus than what we just looked at. It has to do with what we choose to see in ourselves and each other.

All of us have a wide range of qualities, tendencies, and potentials inside ourselves. We're all a mixed bag of love and hatred, strength and weakness, ignorance and wisdom. One of the most powerful influences on what grows within us is what gets support, emphasis, or *belief* – both from us, and also from those who surround us. We actually have what are called "mirror neurons" in our brains that pick up and tend to mirror what others perceive and how they respond. When those close to us believe in us and think we'll succeed, we have a remarkable tendency to meet their expectations. When they believe we're bound to fail or rotten to the core, our path is made dramatically more difficult.

We can think of the potentials that lie within each of us as "seeds" that get watered by our own thoughts and actions, and by the thoughts and actions of others. To love someone is to water the seeds of goodness, joy and confidence within them. It is to see and believe in the best in them, and to express this faith through our thoughts, words and actions.

If we love someone deeply, we become a fierce, unshakeable voice that stares them straight in the eye and says "even if the whole world rejects you or loses faith in you, *I believe in you.* I believe in what's best in you, in your greatest promise and potential. I believe that you can prevail in the challenges of your life, and I am *never, ever giving up on you.*"

Unconditional Love

To put it another way, we decide what's real and true about each other. If my love for you is always dependent on how you *do*, the success you achieve, and so on, then my love is worth very little. If my love sees the goodness and potential at your core and chooses to make that the most important thing, then I can provide real support through life's changes. If we can both do that for each other, then we have something very special: a true gift of love.

Of course, this kind of mutual support is very different from what some of us experienced as we were growing up. But if you learn to offer it to the people in your life, you'll know what it means to be a true friend, and you'll reap the fruits of true friendship. If you do it with those closest to you, then you'll know the beginnings of true intimacy. This is the foundation of unconditional love. It doesn't mean you'll always want to be around someone regardless of how they behave. It just means that you'll continue to love who they are at their core, no matter what. Again, this may or may not be what you're used to, but it's never too late to start.

Pretzel Logic

When I was about five years old, I was playing kickball with a group of kids in my neighborhood. After we'd been playing a while, the woman who lived at the end of the block came outside and asked if we'd help clean up the leaves outside her house. What she actually said was "hey, I'll give each of you kids a big pretzel if you'll clean up these leaves out here and carry them to the back yard."

The other kids were all very nice and started walking toward the woman's house to help. I, on the other hand, stopped a moment, considered that there was a whole bag of pretzels at home, shrugged my shoulders and walked back to my house. The woman glared at me fiercely: I was the evil kid on the block that day. The irony was that I was usually the first one to pitch in when someone asked for help. If she had said: "Hey, can you kids help me with these leaves?" I would have jumped to the front of the line. But I did the calculation, figured the offer was bogus, and went off to gorge myself on pretzels. I can think of better ways of handling the situation now, but hey, I was five, so I give myself a break.

Love is Its Own Reward

The pretzel story might sound trivial, but it actually points to a very real social epidemic. At almost every level of human relationship, life has become increasingly "transactional." It's seen as a transaction between fundamentally separate, self-interested players. We raise our kids based on reward and punishment: "I'll give you this if you're good; you're gonna get *that* if you're bad." In the business world, we're obligated to maximize our return on investment. In civic life and politics, we have to convince people to vote for something because it'll benefit their pocketbook. And while religion preaches love out of one side of its mouth, there's no greater briber on the face of the earth than organized religion.

All of this is the polar opposite of love. In fact, it actually squeezes the habit of love right out of us. Love is its own reward, and anything that makes it about something else undermines its true power.

I'm not suggesting being passive as a parent or in other relationships, doing bad business deals, or ignoring the practical ramifications of political decisions. What I am suggesting is that love raises children differently, establishes different standards for doing business, and has huge implications for a kind of politics that educates the human spirit even as it takes care of practicalities.

Love has even more striking – maybe even heretical – implications for religion. We'll look at all this in later chapters. Here we want to continue exploring some personal, practical ways of building love as a habit of the heart.

Love Doesn't Keep Score

In my first book, *Living Joy*, I give an example of one habit that's especially good at short-circuiting love and messing up our relationships. The example fits well here, so I'd like to paraphrase it for you.[1]

Imagine for a moment that you've got an eight-year-old daughter, and the two of you go to the store late one Sunday afternoon to buy an inflatable ball to take to the beach. As it turns out, there's a big, beautiful ball on sale: instead of $11.99, it's only 8.99. Unfortunately, the register rings up $11.99. You show the clerk the sale sign, but he still insists on charging you $11.99. He's wrong, inept, and stubborn, so you ask him to get the store manager.

Meanwhile, your daughter is standing at the register with you. It's already been twenty minutes, and there's not much daylight left. You get increasingly frustrated standing under the harsh lights waiting for the manager to finish with someone else. Eventually, the manager arrives. She corrects the situation, apologizes, and gives you the sale price. You and your daughter walk out an hour after you first entered the store. You were right, the sales clerk was wrong, and now there's barely any light left at the beach. You play for ten minutes, then head home.

This is life for a lot of us — especially in our most intimate relationships. We get stuck at the cash register, making sure we aren't getting swindled, and we never get our day in the sun together. Not only that, but we're also lousy accountants. We always notice what we do for the other person, but often fail to notice or remember what they do for us. Many a struggling relationship has been redeemed when one person unilaterally stops

---

1   *Several passages from Living Joy have been adapted for use in the Gift of Love. Although the two books develop in very different directions, they share a common starting point and overlap in subjects related to love.*

keeping track and just starts loving. The whole cycle often shifts from scarcity and haggling to abundance and overflowing love.

To be clear, I'm not suggesting that you deny your own needs, or become a doormat for people to walk all over. I just mean that you don't have to constantly be on guard protecting your interests and haggling about who gets what. Truth be told, no one ever really got their needs met that way anyway. They just turn their entire lives into a protracted negotiation session. Nothing could be sadder. As my old friend Hafiz says:

> *Even after all this time*
> *the sun never says to the earth:*
> *you owe me.*
> *Look what happens*
> *with a love like that —*
> *it lights the whole sky.*
> ~*Hafiz, Daniel Ladinsky translation*~

The Sharing of Gifts

Even when we're involved in a process of exchange with others, the flavor of it can be very different than the grim interaction that many of us have been trained to settle for. When we talk about the *gift* of love, it's not just an empty expression. First and foremost, love is a gift to those who give it. It's a natural expression of your connection to life, and again, it benefits you before it does anything for anyone else.

Secondly, there's another important sense in which love and gifts are connected. It has to do with the actual process of giving something tangible. In the act of giving gifts, we actually tap into a profound form of human interaction that has sacred origins in many cultures spanning back thousands of years. The deeper meaning is often lost in our own time, but there's no reason we can't resurrect it.

Let's say you give someone roses. If you give the person roses because you expect something in return, you both lose out. If the other person thinks she's now obligated in any way, she can't fully enjoy the flowers. If you interpret it that way, it's a bribe, not a gift, and you miss out on the delight of giving freely.

To give freely is to trust that there's enough to go around, that all you need will enter your life in its own time and in its own way. This requires focus. You focus on loving, and you get to experience the kind of connection that only comes when you aren't calculating who gets what.

When you give freely for the sheer joy of giving, it actually breeds a sense of security and abundance. It chops away at the mindset of scarcity and cutthroat competition that poisons the common well and turns us all into spiritual paupers no matter how much money and possessions we have.

On Receiving

Equally important is the art of receiving. I remember going to dinner once with a woman named Anna (not her real name). Anna had very little money, and her friends would often take her out for dinner, drinks or entertainment. Anna is a lovely woman, and she has a very deep spiritual orientation. Because of her strong view that God is the source of everything, she makes a practice of never saying thank you when someone treats her. It's an interesting approach, and there may be truth in it, but I think it misses something important.

The moment we say thank you can actually be very special. We might say it like a machine or mumble it politely, but it can be much more meaningful than that. If you actually stop for a moment and thank someone with real presence and your whole heart, things have a way of coming alive. It's not just "thank you" at the checkout stand as though the person hardly exists on your way to more important things. It becomes something like "thank you to all the people in my life, and all the ways you support me." "Thank you to those who have supported me in the past so that I can be here now." "Thank you for the sun, the water, the air and the earth." "Thank you for all that's been given to me that others may not be fortunate enough to have." "Thank you for the gift of being alive."

When you say stuff like that — out-loud or to yourself — the impact on your state of mind can be very powerful. It may sound too flowery or overblown when you just read it here, but if you actually stop and say thank you with real presence, it can trigger a very palpable sense of gratitude and heightened awareness.

Finally, whether you're giving or receiving, there's one reflection that really brings the experience of gratitude alive. Simply remember the fact that each and every time you see someone, it may be the very last time you see them. Reflect on that. Really let it sink in. Remind yourself of it often: "This may be the last time." And then *celebrate*. What else, really, is worth doing?

As Essential as Life Itself

We've looked now at a few small, everyday interactions that give us the opportunity to practice gratitude and to cultivate our capacity for love. But we shouldn't leave things sounding too nice and fluffy. If you're living in the midst of real human desperation – a war zone, genocide, or terror for example – the demands of love are undoubtedly very different and vastly greater. Yet even there, the stakes involved in small expressions of human camaraderie are actually much higher than they may seem.

One of the most famous books ever written is Viktor Frankl's *Man's Search for Meaning*. It's Frankl's account of his experience surviving life in a concentration camp during the Holocaust. Wise, agonizing, and inspiring, the book looks at how people survive, both physically and emotionally, under the worst imaginable conditions.

To me the single most *surprising* passage of the entire book is where Frankl recounts something seemingly very "light." Frankl tells the story of impromptu "cabaret" sessions that prisoners were sometimes able to organize. The sessions typically included a few songs, poems, jokes, or a brief skit. Living right on the brink of death by starvation and torture, you might think that something like a few minutes of music or comedy would be totally irrelevant. What's especially amazing is that Frankl recalls how some prisoners, though they were living on the very brink of starvation, would actually skip a meal to be able to attend one of the sessions.

Do you feel the significance of that? We live in a world that habitually discounts anything that can't be weighed and measured. The mainstream of modern culture tells us that anything pertaining to the human spirit is somehow less real than the stuff we can calculate in grams and ounces and dollars and cents. But love is not a luxury. It is the essential redeeming spirit of life. In fact, when love is lost, nothing else matters. And you are the one – no one else – who determines the part that love will play in your life.

Chapter Three:
Effective Self-Care

You Are Worthy of Love

We've looked now at how we can gain a sense of ease and freedom by focusing our attention on love for others. It would be a mistake, though, to imagine that loving others somehow means denying oneself. If other people deserve your love, why shouldn't you? Whatever any of us may have done in the past, whatever our seeming failings, we all deserve to be loved and cared for. The idea of trying to love everyone except yourself is really kind of silly anyway, isn't it?

Because you have to live with yourself, you probably know your own foibles better than anyone else does (except maybe your spouse or partner – we all know how *that* goes). Especially if you hold yourself to a higher standard than you hold others to, it can be hard to find self-acceptance or to feel worthy. But the truth is that there's no one who deserves your love more than you do. It's really a subtle kind of vanity to think otherwise, as though you should somehow be so different.

Obviously, self-care isn't the same as being obnoxiously self-interested. That never led anyone to happiness. But it also doesn't mean denying yourself or being overly self-critical. It's natural that feelings of self-doubt, remorse, or vulnerability may come up at times. In and of themselves, they may just be a kind of tenderness, or a healthy dose of humility. But they don't need to be indulged or used as an excuse for self-hatred or self-denial.

Above all, you don't have to believe whatever stories your mind might conjure up about *why* you're not worthy. Self-sabotaging thoughts can be very seductive, but the moment you recognize

them as mere stories in the mind, they immediately begin to lose
their spell over you.

The World Needs Your Joy

In actual practice, the more you're able to love and accept yourself, the more your heart can genuinely open to others. There
was a time when the very idea of "self-love" sounded to me like
self-absorption or narcissism. In fact, real self-love is the very
opposite of self-absorption, but only if it's properly understood
and lived. First and foremost that means realizing that your ability
to contribute to anyone else is very closely tied to your ability to
take good care of yourself.

We began *The Gift of Love* by exploring how the choice to
courageously love others can foster your own well being. But it
also works the opposite way. By taking good care of yourself, you
naturally serve others. After all, if you *don't* care for yourself, how
can you expect to help anyone else? If your own life is an exercise
in self-destruction or self-loathing, how can it *not* have a negative
impact on those around you? If you're stressed and miserable,
stress and misery is what you're very likely to create.

Likewise, if you're kind and wise toward yourself, if you're
clear and joyful, joy and clarity are what you're most likely to
create. A lot of us work hard to help others. But as much as the
world needs your work, *it needs your joy at least as much.* If you really
want to make meaningful contributions to others, it's critical to
realize that your state of being dramatically affects the outcomes
that you achieve. So if you want to help others, effective self-care

belongs right at the top of your list of priorities. It may not be the only thing up there, but it at least deserves a share of the limelight. Otherwise, you're like a person trying to save someone from drowning while you're drowning yourself. I've tried it, and it's not very effective.

Two Kinds of Caring

Here's another way to clarify what healthy self-love really means. Put simply, the vast majority of human beings care way too much *about* themselves, and way too little *for* themselves.

When you care a lot *about* yourself, you're constantly worried about outcomes: about how your health, finances, love life and family life will turn out, about all cliffhanging twists and turns of your personal story. Your worry might range from mildly preoccupied to downright obsessed. On the obsessed end of the scale, every moment that things go your way is taken as a sign that life is as it should be, and every moment that things don't go your way is taken as a disaster. To care tremendously about yourself is to allow the habit of ego to tyrannize your life. It is *the story of you getting lost in the story of you,* and it creates tremendous unnecessary suffering.

When you care *for* yourself, you focus on the present instead of getting stuck in regrets about the past or worries about the future. In fact, it's only by taking care of the present that you *can* take care of the future. You treat yourself kindly and wisely, cultivating the skills that truly support your well-being, which in turn supports the well-being of those whose lives you touch.

So imagine for a moment not caring quite so much how it all goes. Though you continue to prefer some things to others, imagine being at peace with whatever unfolds. Unhook yourself from the next twist or turn in the plot as though it were *all so tremendously important*. See yourself finding ways to take superb care of yourself – physically, emotionally, spiritually, in your relationships and in all the dimensions of your life. Imagine being really kind to yourself, really strong, really *free*. That's the taste of it.

Re-parenting Yourself

So what does self-care really mean in a practical sense? How do you actually do it? A good way to start is to recognize that different parts of you are involved. One part has to care for another. If you're hammering a nail, and you slip and bash your left thumb, your right hand takes care of the thumb by putting ice on it. Your aching left thumb can't do the job itself; it needs some help. The same is true with the rest of your body, and your emotions as well. There are parts that need tending, and parts that are capable of being strong, wise, and caring.

You can think of the part that needs tending as though it were a young child, and the wise, strong part as though it were a very skilled parent. This is a popular concept in contemporary psychology. Though it may be overused at times, it's actually an apt metaphor for something that's built right into the physiology of your brain and body.

However great or awful your childhood may have been, you received some level of nurturance and care – at least enough to make it here. And you also received some wounding – enough to make you tender in places. All of this lives on in the physiology of your brain and body, especially in what's called the "limbic system" – the emotional brain and body. And all of it can be changed by bringing a new kind of "self-parenting" to your experience. Rather than dwelling too intently on what happened in the past, you can actually transform the patterns of your thoughts, emotions and daily life by caring for yourself in the present. The change may be dramatic, or it may be very subtle and gradual. Either way, it can make a powerful difference in your capacity for wellness and contentment.

What Do You Feel?

Self-care begins, first and foremost, with awareness. If you're not even aware of what's going on, it's just about impossible to effectively respond. Let's say a mother is sitting with her baby in very hot or very cold weather. Her baby may be bitterly cold or sweltering in the heat, but if she has no awareness of what the baby is feeling, how can she possibly take care of the baby's needs?

It's the same with you. If you have no awareness of what you feel – physically and emotionally – you can't begin to take really good care of yourself. So step one is to bring awareness to your emotional state by simply asking yourself: *"What do I feel?"* You can try it now. Just pause for a moment, and ask yourself: *What am I feeling physically?* Do you feel heat, coolness, pressure? Do you feel the sensation of your breath entering and leaving your body? And then: *what am I feeling emotionally?* Is the feeling glad?

Sad? Mad? Curious? Neutral? Just take a moment to check in with yourself. As you make a habit of checking in on what you feel, the awareness of your emotions increasingly becomes second nature.

Responsibility and Freedom

Not only does this kind of emotional awareness bring a dose of reality; it also brings a dose of responsibility. When a young child cries and throws a tantrum, its anger usually gets directed at whoever's in shouting distance. Adults may be more sophisticated in how we project our anger, but that just makes us big, sophisticated babies.

If I say "you're such a *#*##," it's really just an escape from the truth, which is that *I'm angry*. As soon as I'm really aware of how I feel — aware enough to name it — there's a bit of freedom in my experience. Instead of blindly relating *from* the emotion, I'm relating *to* it from a larger space of awareness. And as soon as I relate to it from awareness, I have a chance to take care of my needs instead of wasting energy blaming and complaining.

What's needed?

Step two in the process of effective self-care is to ask yourself what's needed in the moment. "Need" here doesn't mean *absolute* need — you need this or you'll die, you need this or the universe will cease to exist. It just means what's helpful — what the situation calls for. Nor is what you need necessarily the same as what you *want*: that could be a pack of cigarettes, a fifth of vodka or a pound of chocolate. When you ask what's needed, you're consulting the wise, discerning part of yourself – the "wise parent" that has the ability to provide helpful guidance.

The moment that you ask what's needed, a very important transition takes place. Awareness ceases to be just a spectator; it becomes an active participant in your life. You become *aware with the ability to respond*. It's the beginning of what, in the work of the Human Fulfillment Institute, we call *"Interactive Awareness."*

Interactive Awareness and the Potential for Freedom

Awareness is a lot like a light. (In fact it's often called "the light of awareness.") Like any other light, the function of awareness is to illuminate whatever it comes in contact with. But imagine if you have a flashlight and always leave it stowed away in a drawer. Even if it has fresh batteries, it's not going to illuminate a whole lot.

Wherever you shine the light of awareness – whatever area of your life awareness starts to illuminate – is an area where you gain a measure of freedom. Whether it's your body, your mind, your emotions or your relationships, the more that things become conscious, the less you can be blindly controlled and victimized by them. Where there's awareness, there's the potential for wisdom and positive change.

The Eight Domains of Experience

It's standard operating procedure these days for most systems of personal and professional development to include at least some awareness of mind, body and emotions. The better, bolder approaches go a step farther and include "spirit," even though the term raises all sorts of questions and turns some people off and means different things to different people.

It's also possible to extend the scope of awareness to include a number of other critically important domains of experience. On a practical level, bringing awareness to these other key areas vastly expands the process of self-care, and makes positive, lasting change a whole lot more likely. The following are what I refer to as the *"Eight Domains"* of Interactive Awareness:

- Mind (cognitive)
- Body (somatic)
- Emotions (emotive)
- Spirit (spiritual)
- Social Environment (interpersonal)
- Physical Environment (environmental)
- Action (proactive)
- Awareness Itself (conscious)

Let's look at how self-care actually works in relation to these domains.

Dynamics of Healing

Let's say I'm someone who suffers from alcoholism, and I want to stop drinking so that I can live a healthier, more fulfilling life. (A very challenging example like this can help us keep things real.) How would awareness of the Eight Domains help me achieve lasting change? Let's look at each domain.

Mind: What ways of thinking have characterized my life up until now? If I'm like most people who suffer from alcoholism, I've probably told myself a variation of one or more of the following:

- "I'm not an alcoholic; I could quit if I really wanted to."
- "I just need to exert more willpower, and then I can quit."
- "It's hopeless; I'll never be able to quit."

To change my situation, all of these ways of thinking will have to go. I'll have to face the reality of my life, believe that change is possible, and avail myself of whatever help I can get to make the changes I need to make.

Body: Whatever my ways of thinking may be, if I suffer from alcoholism, I'll need to deal with the physical aspects of the addiction. In the short term, this will involve a biological process of withdrawal. In the medium and long term, it may involve new ways of relating to my body with respect to exercise, nutrition, and other basic components of physical self-care.

Emotions: What are the emotional needs that drinking has covered up until now? I'll need to learn effective ways of practicing emotional self-care if my life is to change. This may include caring for myself in ways that parents and others might have failed to, and also asking others for appropriate kinds of support.

Spirit: Whatever my spiritual inclinations or lack thereof, I'm going to need to find some greater sense of purpose, belonging, and/or a larger order of things that I belong to. It may or may not be in the form that "twelve-step" groups typically emphasize, but it will almost certainly include some source of power greater than personal willpower if I'm ever going to make lasting change.

Social and Physical Environment: Among the most important ways that I practice mental, emotional, physical and spiritual self-care will be the quality of my relationships, and where I actually spend my time. If I try to make changes internally, but keep playing pool with my drinking buddies at the corner bar, it's extremely unlikely that anything will really change. I may have to leave toxic relationships behind, and learn to do relationships differently. I may need to learn to make appropriate requests for support, and also offer support in new ways, so that genuine mutual support becomes the foundation of all my close relationships.

Awareness and Action: Awareness will be at the core of all of these changes, and action is what will make them real. Actions that are repeated become habits, and habits are largely what direct the course of our lives. Put bluntly, it's a waste of time to talk about love, wisdom, or fulfillment without digging into the real-life habits that shape our lives. This is where the rubber hits the road. It's the last and juiciest subject for us to look at under the topic of self-care.

Self-Care Habits

Let's put ourselves on the hot seat for a moment. You pick up a book called *The Gift of Love,* spend a few hours with it, and maybe you come out with a few worthwhile thoughts or insights to carry with you when you're done reading. But what would it take for this to be the moment that you reach a true turning point in your life? What would it take for your experience of love to actually deepen so significantly and in such a way that the very trajectory of your life shifts for good?

To put it another way, how can you change long-established habits? Even if you gain some kind of insight, patterns of negative thinking and behavior are usually deeply ingrained and tend to go on despite whatever momentary "ahas" you might enjoy in the moment. How can you actually build lasting habits of positive thought, feeling and action into your mind and heart and life?

One way is through immersion: if you have the time and resources to immerse yourself in a workshop or retreat, that can be an excellent way to initiate new and positive changes in areas that you want to develop. It helps tremendously to put yourself in a different environment that can help shake loose old habits and circumstances.

But even then, seemingly profound changes in the context of an intensive event often have a way of fading afterwards, as the old habits and circumstances of life return. In fact, it's not uncommon for people to swear that their lives are dramatically changed forever after a workshop, retreat, or some intense, unplanned life experience — only to crash in despair when all the big changes seem to dissolve before their eyes a few short days or weeks later.

Support Options

So how to make positive life changes really stick? Some of us have grappled with this question for years. Here are a few options that you might consider. If you start looking into some of these support structures *during the time that you're reading this book*, you can set patterns in motion that may make a lasting difference in your life.

Natural Networks. The most effective support structures are often those that are naturally occurring and face-to-face: networks of friendship, fellowship and community. One of the best ways to strengthen these bonds is something very simple: offering and asking for help. Asking a friend for advice with a decision, offering to help a family member with a small task, even taking time out for a quick interaction at the grocery store can be an opportunity to cultivate this critically important skill and habit.

On the other hand, the limitation of these naturally occurring connections is that they may lack sustained focus in a particular area that you want to develop. Building support for an exercise or nutritional program, for example, usually is not a one shot deal. Additionally, the very familiarity of existing relationships with family and friends can cut both ways. Remember those "mirror neurons" that tend to lock us into people's perceptions and expectations? Sometimes it takes breaking out of your existing social circle to chart a new course.

Psychotherapy, Coaching and Consulting. Whereas friendship is defined by mutuality and reciprocity (you help each other out), the job of a life coach or therapist is purely to be there for you. He or she is paid to bring unique skills to bear on your situation and to call forth your own wisdom and resourcefulness. The direct one-on-one format of the relationship is both its strength and its limitation. It can play a very important role in helping you to see and move beyond unwanted patterns in your life. At the same time, for lasting change to take root, the circle of support and connection usually has to grow much broader than a one- on- one appointment each week or two.

Support Groups. These can be small groups that meet in person or online. The latter lack face-to-face contact, which is a significant drawback, but they do have the benefit of being quickly accessible. In fact, various organizations, from social and professional networks to political campaigns have discovered that people who first interact online can often be moved to take real-life, real-world action together. Social networking sites provide a useful tool for this. However, it's usually very difficult to create coherent, focused support networks using social networking alone. See what works for you – is there a support group of some sort that appeals to you? What might actually help you follow through in the areas where you'd most like to make progress?

Topical Courses. One of the best ways to connect with other people to make lasting change is in the context of an ongoing course. Whether it's an exercise class, a course on financial habits, or a program on effective self-care, topical courses can provide structure, focus, and social support that can otherwise be hard to come by. [2]

Whichever support options you choose to explore, the most important thing is that you make self-care a high, daily priority. As you cultivate effective ways of caring *for* yourself instead of caring too much *about* yourself, you'll soon experience real and positive change. Self-love will become a practical reality instead of an empty ideology.

Having given yourself the gift of self-care, the next step is to broaden the scope of love. To do that, we'll wrestle a bit with that word we just used – "ideology." Though it's often well-intended, ideology – also known in its more rigid forms as *dogma* – is the prime villain in our plot, the number one adversary of love.

And it always helps to know your adversaries if you want to kick their butts.

---

2   *A number of courses and other resources specifically related to self-care and positive habit-building can be found on the Renewal Space website at www.renewalspace.net.*

Chapter Four:
Expanding The Circle

Natural Empathy

It's a cold winter morning, and Janice Brown is getting ready to take her four-year-old son Sammy for a walk. Standing on the front porch, Janice leans over to put gloves on Sammy's hands. She doesn't have to think about it. She doesn't have to calculate the temperature or ask Sammy how his hands feel. It's instinctive. Janet puts gloves on her son's hands as though they were her own.

This is the natural expression of empathetic love. It's as natural as the sunlight that makes plants grow. Our ability to feel and express empathy can be cultivated as a skill and a habit, but we don't cultivate it by adding something artificial. We cultivate it by uncovering our natural sense of care and connection.

The real question is what gets in the way of our natural empathetic response? What is it that shuts down our capacity for love, or keeps it from ripening? We might sense barriers to love in our feelings or circumstances. When we're grouchy, frightened or confused, it's certainly harder to be loving towards others. Likewise, if we've had a tough day filled with seemingly aggravating people and events, our capacity for love can be put to the test.

But what most powerfully affects our ability to love over the long run isn't merely our feelings or the events in our lives. It's most often our *beliefs*. Perhaps more than any other factor, it is our beliefs that either open or close the doors of our hearts to love.

Ideologies of *Me*

When I was growing up, my mother would sometimes explain her decision to do something selfish by sternly proclaiming: "Well, I'm no female Jesus Christ!" It was her way of expressing what we could call an *Ideology of Me* — a rationale that justifies why we not only *are* selfish, but why we *should* be selfish, why it's *good, right* or *natural* for us to be selfish. (And, of course, by selfish here, we don't mean self-care, but a lack of care for others.)

Here are some of the beliefs that often make up an Ideology of Me:

- "I've got enough of my own problems without worrying about anyone else."
- "People are biologically hardwired to be selfish. It's a fact of human nature."
- "The world is a place of scarcity and competition for scarce resources is the natural state of affairs."
- "Financial worth defines self-worth."
- "Greed is good."
- "If everyone pursues their own self-interest, it actually turns out best for everyone."
- "It's best to mistrust people until they prove worthy of your trust."
- "There are winners and losers in life, and winning is what matters most."
- "Always look out for Number One."

- "You have to be realistic."
- "People never really change."
- "Nothing in the world ever really changes."
- "There's no point swimming against the tide."
- "Selfishness is sexy."

Whether spoken out loud or held as assumptions, these kinds of beliefs can powerfully shape our experience. Indeed, they can easily become self-fulfilling prophecies. There are actually two very famous physicists named David Bohm and Karl Pribram who have suggested that our thoughts may function on subatomic levels in such a way that they directly affect external physical realities. If so, the impact of our attitudes and perspectives may extend farther than we can rationally fathom. Metaphysical ideas about the so-called "Law of Attraction" have long held this to be true. But even short of any direct effects on the physical world, there's a powerful, well-established psychological process that makes our beliefs extremely potent. It's called *"Confirmation Bias."*

Confirmation Bias is the tendency of the mind to *only allow information that confirms one's existing opinion.* It is a formidable, empirically verifiable phenomenon that reaches its zenith in the form of ideology and dogma. The more we believe something to be true, the more our experience will seem to confirm it. And the more emotionally attached to the belief we are, the more likely we are to blind ourselves to anything that doesn't fit or that might threaten to undo our initial opinion.

Empowering Beliefs

On the opposite side of the spectrum are ideas that tend to create a world of connection and alignment. For example:

- "Most people are fundamentally good when given a chance."
- "No one is an island: we're all connected."
- "The greatest blessing in life isn't what you get; it's what you give."
- "A successful life isn't about getting dealt the best hand; it's what you do with the cards you're dealt."
- "Integrity and positive intentions matter more than outward rewards."
- "However good or bad the situation seems, there's always an opportunity to meet the situation with the best that's within you."
- "When sorrows are shared, they're easier to bear. When joys are shared, they're made greater."
- "I have so many blessings in my life. How did I get to be so lucky?"
- "Whatever the next challenge that I face, I'll handle it."
- "Life is amazingly abundant. It has a way of taking care of what needs to be taken care of.
- "What goes around comes around, especially when it comes to love."

Once again, when you adopt these kinds of beliefs and attitudes, the world has a remarkable way of organizing itself around your frame of mind. Life reflects your thoughts, feelings and expectations, almost like a movie screen reflects the images that are projected onto it.

Consciousness of We

So the basic thing we're watching for is how your beliefs might affect your ability to experience and express love. Not surprisingly, the first place this usually shows up is with those closest to you. When the premise of your relationships is a belief in abundance, generosity, connection and love, you live in a world of "win-win," and harmony becomes possible. When you habitually compare, compete, and calculate who's getting what, it's easy to feel shortchanged.

As we've noted, we tend to notice what we do for others, but may not notice or remember what they do for us. That's why in most relationships, if you figure you give about seventy per cent and receive about thirty per cent, you're probably about even. The bigger shift is really to not calculate so much, to think more in terms of *we* rather than just *you* or *me*.

When you think in terms of *we*, you don't have to worry so incessantly about who's getting what. Life can be more collaborative and less transactional, because you're part of a team – of a larger whole.

Our First Circle of Influence

Whatever beliefs you adopt will determine what you take to be "reality," and will set the limits of love in your life. This is especially true of beliefs you hold so close that you aren't even aware of them.

But it's especially important to remember that making love *real* begins with those nearest to us. If we can't do it with family, friends and others in our immediate environment, it makes no sense to start talking about love for the world, or for people we don't know. Loving everyone in general but no one in particular is just abstract spiritual BS.

These days, with so many forces that tend to uproot us, it can actually be a great challenge to create and maintain stable, healthy bonds with family and close friends. But it's tremendously important. For most of us, it will determine the quality of our lives as much or more than whatever personal or professional projects we take on. We have to stop the forward momentum of our lives and tyranny of our to-do lists enough to be really present for those close to us, to make them our priority, and to bring them the best of what we have to offer.

The Wisdom of Cowboy Mike

Making love real usually begins with family and friends, but it surely doesn't end there. A number of years ago, I was riding on a train in Alaska, and I met an old cowboy named Mike. Mike had leathery, weather-beaten skin, stubbly grey whiskers, gleaming blue eyes, and the kind of wizened smile that you only see on people who have been around a long time, and who have seen and learned a lot.

Mike and I got to talking, and I asked him what lessons he had learned in his life. He gave just one answer: "to break bread with different kinds of people." To him, that was the key to keeping life fresh, and to discovering the real meaning of love and understanding.

It's actually interesting that Mike used the phrase "breaking bread." Our word "company" comes from *"com"* and *"pani"* – the sharing of bread. Some anthropologists believe that's why humans first started walking on two legs – so we could carry food to each other. I wonder what Mike, out there with the grizzlies and caribou and salmon (and occasional human) would think about that.

For a lot of us, though, breaking bread with different kinds of people can actually be a pretty big stretch. We tend to live our lives in fairly small concentric circles. There are family members or friends we're closest to. Then there are more casual friends, acquaintances, community members, and other people with whom we may share some particular history or mutual interest. And that's about as far as our habit-zone or comfort-zone usually goes.

There's nothing wrong with connecting to like-minded people, and we're lucky indeed if we have a tight-knit circle of family or close friends. But the circle of love in our lives can grow much wider. Put bluntly, if I say my life or my love is *just* for family or those closest to me, or even if I limit it to my community or my country, I haven't become fully human. To be fully human means that I have the ability to put myself in the shoes of others. It means that I can care for those who may be very different or very far away.

Expanding The Circle

Truth be told, our inability to identify and empathize with those who are different or distant underlies many of the world's greatest ills. Whether we're talking about street violence, warfare, modern-day slavery, oppression of ethnic or religious groups, subjugation of women, repression of civil and political freedoms, or ecological devastation, a similar dynamic is at work. And each of us is connected to these larger issues in ways that might not initially meet the eye.

Before we point our finger at who's to blame for the world's woes (which is, after all, so easy to do), perhaps we can first summon the courage to look inward. Here are some questions we might ask ourselves:

- In what ways do I limit my experience and expression of love?
- What beliefs or stories do I tell myself that prevent me from loving more broadly?
- How can I connect to people beyond my usual circle?
- Who can I break bread with that I haven't broken bread with before?
- Is there one simple act of love I can take that takes *me* out of my comfort zone?

By expressing love in new and broader ways, each of us can grow a larger, more beautiful, more fulfilling life. And even if the actions we undertake seem very small, their power to make a difference can be surprising. You never know where they might lead. A woman in Montgomery, Alabama decides she won't follow orders to sit at the back of a bus, and an entire era of civil rights is unleashed in the United States. A feisty former attorney in Calcutta, India goes on a hunger strike and by sheer force of example quells riots that thousands of armed troops can't suppress. Of course, Rosa Parks and Mohandas Gandhi were no ordinary people. But maybe you aren't either. You never know how things might unfold, what one small change in your own life might bring about in the world.

Besides, how would we keep score, anyway? Perhaps you've heard the story of the man who comes upon a young boy standing at the seashore, tossing starfish back into the sea. The man asks the boy what he's doing – doesn't he realize that thousands of fish all up and down the shore got stranded when the tide went out, that he can't possibly make a difference? Throwing another starfish back, the boy looks up and smiles: "It made a difference to that one."

Let's not fail to do what we can because we're preoccupied with what we can't.

Love and Money

In seeking to expand the "circle of care" in our lives, one of the first obstacles we often confront comes the moment we start dealing with anything related to money and possessions. Our relationship to money and material possessions taps into our basic survival instincts, our felt need for security, and our sense of self-worth.

It also rubs up against issues of personal power and sexuality. Jane may feel attracted to John's wealth because she feels it can provide security, or can buy beautiful things that help her feel beautiful. John may feel powerful, successful or virile with a new sports car parked in his driveway. In either case, the real prize is something much less tangible than the physical objects themselves.

In fact, if you look deeply enough at what drives your desire for something material, you may find that it actually has something to do, however indirectly, with a desire for love and connection. Especially in our time and culture, where a lot of the historical bonds of family and community have been frayed, material possessions often serve as substitutes for love, connection, community, and a basic "joie de vivre" or sense of celebration.

Materialism can easily become addictive, and like most addictions, the problem is that you can never get enough of what you don't really want. You can drink fine wine and eat great food and visit exotic places, and still end out totally miserable. You can keep consuming and accumulating more and more stuff, but it doesn't really help for very long because what you really want is something that exists on a completely different level of reality.

I used to have a rat in my garage that would eat through absolutely anything. The messes it left behind were truly ugly, but I have to admit I was kind of impressed by how ravenous and powerful the critter was. I think back on times when I've tried to fill the need for love and connection by buying or consuming something, and I think I wasn't much different from the rat. I probably could have devoured the entire planet and still not felt satisfied.

The Art of Savoring

None of this is to say that we shouldn't enjoy nice things. On the contrary, if we really slow down and savor our enjoyments, they're much more likely to feel truly fulfilling instead of addictive. If we can taste the food on our plate each meal with the same quality of attention that we would give to a hundred dollar glass of wine, we'll know what it means to feel nourished. If we can sip *all* of life's joys like that, we'll nourish ourselves in very deep and lasting ways. Something as simple as taking a walk, or even taking a breath, can be a source of true joy.

And why stop there? If we can celebrate the first moment of each day that we see someone we love as a greater fortune than winning the lottery – which it surely is – then we'll begin to know what it means to be truly happy.

The basic point is simply that we need not let our relationship to money and things hijack our capacity for love. Only love can give us the sources of joy that we truly long for. That isn't some sweet romantic ideal; it's reality. The more we get in touch with that reality, the more we find fulfillment. And the more we find fulfillment, the more it spills over to everyone whose lives we touch.

Chapter Five:
The Power Of Compassion

First-Order Compassion

Love's greatest power often reveals itself in the face of suffering. Loving response to suffering is what I mean by the term *compassion*. We can feel and express compassion in response to our own suffering, the suffering of others, and the suffering of the world itself.

Compassion is the natural response of an open heart; it's not something that you can *force* yourself or anyone else to experience. Compassion becomes possible whenever we have the courage to open ourselves to life's sorrows and tragedies — when we let ourselves truly see and feel the pain of life rather than closing our eyes or heart.

I remember walking down the streets of Calcutta, seeing people with all sorts of deformities begging. One person I will never forget was a legless beggar who was rolling down the sidewalk, clanking his begging cup against the pavement. It was hard to witness that level of poverty, and at the same time, it was very valuable for someone coming from an affluent nation to experience. Among other things, it revealed the difference between compassion and pity.

As I use the term, pity feels suffering and despairs in it. Pity has a way of remaining separate from those who are suffering, and even subtly holding them down. By contrast, compassion is empowering: it feels suffering, but doesn't lose sight of people's humanity and potential. You may feel shocked seeing a legless beggar rolling down the sidewalk, but you also feel connected in your common humanity, and you may even feel respect for the man's resourcefulness and determination. With compassion, it becomes possible to see beneath the surface of the situation, to the strength of the human spirit that shines at the core.

The ability to feel and constructively respond to suffering is one of our most essential human attributes. Nothing, I believe, contributes more to living a truly well-lived life. There's one place, though, where compassion is really put to the test. It's in the way that we respond to those who have suffered at the hands of others — those who have been victimized in one way or another. It's an arena where the stakes can be very high, and it comes with its own special challenges.

To experience and express compassion for those who have been wronged requires that we have at least some capacity to feel the pain and anger that they feel, that we have an appropriate respect for its depth, and that we not try to excuse, fix, or sugar-coat it in any way. Compassion for those who suffer is what I call *First-Order Compassion*. Only when we've fully felt and responded to this first great calling of compassion can we begin to respond to what I refer to as *Second-Order Compassion*.

Second-Order Compassion

Second-Order Compassion is among the greatest challenges of the human spirit. It is rare, and it is difficult. Second-Order Compassion responds with love not only to those who suffer, but even to those who *inflict* suffering. This can't be approached as some sweet, Pollyanna notion that glazes over reality. On the contrary, it is the fiercest, most demanding calling that love can make upon us. And it can only be approached when the first challenge of compassion has been fully met.

Whether we're responding to someone who harms us personally, or someone who inflicts suffering on others, our capacity for love is put to its greatest test. If the suffering they inflict is substantial, if their motives are genuinely cruel or calloused, or even if they're just profoundly ignorant, we may have to experience tremendous anger before we can discover anything else. We may even have to experience what can only be described as hatred, or a desire for retribution. These are powerful human impulses, and they need to be given their due before we can practice genuine forgiveness or compassion. That doesn't mean we have to *act* on hatred or indulge in it. It just means that we need to honestly meet the reality of our experience rather than repressing it or glossing it over with niceties.

If we're counseling *someone else* to respond with compassion and forgiveness, we need to tread even more carefully. Shortly after the attacks of September11, I remember watching actor Richard Gere make a presentation before a large audience of New Yorkers. Gere was talking about the brutality of the attacks, and he urged people to respond with compassion rather than vengeance. The suffering in the wake of the attacks was still very fresh in people's hearts, and I remember the crowd of New York City firefighters and others roundly booing his comments.

Gere accepted the crowd's response with admirable grace and patience, but to me, the event revealed the importance of timing, and of clearly meeting the requirements of First-Order Compassion before trying to open the door to the Second. You have to truly meet people's suffering before you can try to do anything with it.

It's also critically important that any talk of compassion, forgiveness, or reconciliation not be confused for an attempt to absolve people of their responsibility. There are all sorts of factors that contribute to human cruelty, greed, dishonesty, and so on. But that doesn't absolve any of us of personal responsibility for our actions. Only when we acknowledge the importance of personal responsibility can we look in earnest at the healing work that love performs in the midst of hatred and violence.

The Legacy of Tariq Khamisa

There are many brilliant examples of Second-Order Compassion shining forth on the world stage. The non-violent movements of Gandhi, King, Mandela, Aung San Suu Kyi, and others immediately come to mind. At other times, the work of Second-Order Compassion is carried out on a more personal level. The following is one such instance.

The date is January 21, 1995, and Tariq Khamisa, a twenty-year-old student at San Diego State University, is working the night shift delivering pizza. When Tariq arrives to make his delivery, he's greeted by a group of young gang members. One of the youngest in the group, a fourteen-year old boy named Tony Hicks, is undergoing a gang rite-of-passage. As planned and instructed, Tony points a gun at Tariq and demands that he hand over the pizzas. Tariq refuses, and starts moving back towards his delivery truck. Tony hesitates, unsure how to respond, and then, prodded by the older gang members, he pulls the trigger. Tariq Khamisa collapses and dies shortly after. Tony Hicks is convicted of first-degree murder and sentenced to life in prison, a sentence which he continues to serve today.

What makes this story exceptional is not the violence or the age of those involved. What makes it exceptional is the series of events that followed in the aftermath of the shooting. When Tariq's father Azim Khamisa first learned of his only son's murder, he said it felt "like a nuclear bomb had gone off" inside his heart. A deeply spiritual man, Azim would then undergo months of what he described as excruciating pain, intense grieving, soul searching, and a determined quest to find some peace, some solace, some way to move on. "The quality of the rest of my life," says Azim, "would hinge on how I handled this tragedy."

What finally emerged from Azim Khamisa's deep mourning and reflection was something much larger than his own personal story. Azim Khamisa came forth with a profound commitment to create something positive and redeeming from his son's tragedy. One of his first decisions was to meet face-to-face with Tony Hicks. When he did, rather than the savage monster that he expected, he found a sensitive, remorseful young man.

Azim also met with Hicks' grandfather, Ples Felix, who had been doing his best to raise Tony in the absence of the boy's mother and abusive father. Azim discovered that Ples was also a man of deep faith, and shared a strong desire to be of service. Ples had been devastated to see Tony change from what he described as a "loving, courteous, well-spoken, very sensitive grandson" into a gang member who shot and killed another young man. Ples was appalled by what gang life had meant for his grandson, and for the son of Azim Khamisa.

With Ples's help, Azim began the The Tariq Khamisa Foundation. Together, they developed an educational program to help young people choose alternatives to violence. Azim and Ples travel around the country together speaking at schools, city halls, recreation centers, and religious organizations. They have personally reached 350,000 children and millions more have heard their story through broadcasts and media publications. I have seen them speak, and they are a powerful, inspiring team. I can only begin to imagine what it would be like to lose a child to violence. Azim Khamisa's choice to respond with love speaks volumes about the redemptive capacity of the human spirit. It is an outstanding example of Second Order Compassion at work in the world.

Hatred as Contagious Disease

The compassion and forgiveness that Azim Khamisa practiced is not something that you can demand of anyone else. But it can certainly provide us with a light to look more clearly into our own lives. How many of us hold grudges, or seek retribution for even the smallest of transgressions? How many of us find it difficult to accept or to love those who are different, or distant, or more successful than we are? (Yes, when we're caught in the world of ego, that third type of person is often among the most difficult for us to love). What kinds of needless "interpersonal litter" do we leave strewn across the landscape of our lives?

Just as the act of love benefits the one who loves before it benefits anyone else, so we are harmed first when we hate. Hatred and true joy can never occupy our attention at the same time – they are polar opposites. Practicing forgiveness and love when we are wronged is not a moral nicety – it is a precondition for our own well being. As Azim Khamisa says, "In one of human nature's strange twists, full healing for the victim may require him or her to grant that forgiveness. There may be no other way to put down the destructive anger."

Think for a moment of someone who sparks anger in you. It may be someone in your personal life, or someone you believe is responsible for causing suffering in the world. This person may seem cruel, arrogant, dishonest, greedy, petty, or belligerent, and when you think of them, you can't stand it. It's as though their behavior carries a kind of negative electrical charge. And when you catch that charge, you feel anger or hatred.

It's very important to see how this process works. Our hatred for *anyone* is not solely the result of the other person's activity, but also of our own *reactivity*. The negative charge of hatred is like a contagious disease that we allow ourselves to contract. It actually binds us to the very things we hate. It causes us to suffer, and almost invariably to create suffering for others as well.

See The Pain Point

> *"If we could read the secret history of our enemies,*
> *we should find in each man's life sorrow and*
> *suffering enough to disarm all hostility."*
> *~Henry Wadsworth Longfellow~*

The "antibody" to the disease of hatred is understanding. Not just any understanding, but a very specific, no-nonsense understanding that is both hard-won and deeply transforming. Again, lest there be any confusion, this understanding *does not in any way* mean that we condone harmful conduct, absolve people of responsibility for their actions, or choose to subject ourselves to the negative behavior of others. Understanding simply means that we have an accurate perception of what's going on and an accurate assessment of what works in dealing with it.

How do we achieve this understanding? First, we look beneath the level of the harmful action or difficult personality, to the fundamental human condition within which each person lives and acts. We begin to see that every action of every human being is in some way, however distorted or confused it may seem, an attempt to achieve happiness and avoid suffering. We begin to recognize the common essence of human struggle, frailty and confusion that lies beneath even the most heinous acts.

Looking deeply, with a sober, compassionate gaze, you may come to see that even the most vicious acts of the bully or tyrant ultimately stem from some form of ignorance or confusion. At first, this may be difficult to believe, but the more deeply you look, the more this truth will reveal itself.

Whenever someone acts in a way that you dislike, practice looking for the "pain point" – the vulnerable, hurting, stressed or fearful place beneath the outward action. Intuitively zero in on this point, like a professional tracker. Make it your target, and realize that just as you want happiness and don't want suffering, so does the other person. Your perception and response will inevitably change as you practice in this way. Once again, this truth does not in any way excuse or "explain away" harmful actions. It simply allows you to see them clearly, and in this clear seeing, your relationship to the situation begins to transform itself.

Learn to Distinguish Between Actions and Actors

A second part of this unique understanding that uproots hatred comes when you learn to distinguish between *actions* and *actors*. You recognize that no human being is a static, fixed entity. Each of us is a fluid process – a mixed bag of fear, love, greed, caring, and every other inclination that colors the human heart. Instead of allowing your mind to lock onto another person as a solid object worthy of your contempt, you see the changing, fluid nature that we all share as living beings.

Even as you may decry a particular action or pattern of actions, you learn to see the universal human spirit and potential that resides beneath those actions. You see beneath the outward personality of the actor to the common humanity, vulnerability and potential that lies underneath.

If you truly succeed in seeing past the level of behavior and personality, whatever aversion or dislike you feel will not harden into hatred. You may be every bit as passionately opposed to a given action, but instead of hating the other person, your "enemy" becomes hatred itself, and even more fundamentally, the ignorance that underlies hatred. Without absolving anyone of responsibility, you see negative forces in the human heart as a kind of disease that can be contracted, rather than a "rottenness to the core." When you learn to see in this way, instead of responding to hatred with more hatred, your heart spontaneously greets hatred with sadness, and an unswerving commitment to love.

There's no question that this commitment demands a lot from us. Practicing genuine love toward that which seems unlovable is perhaps the single most difficult, courageous act of the human spirit. It signifies neither weakness nor sentimentality. It requires that we break the cycle of reaction within our hearts, shed light on the darkness of ignorance, and chart a new course of freedom in the world.

Ultimately, we come to realize that "evil" acts fundamentally stem from a failure to see the unity of life. When we get transfixed by people's harmful actions, when we fail to see the inherent worthiness of the people themselves, we're actually making the same root mistake that they've made. We're reinforcing the very same divided consciousness that breeds the evil that we deplore. When we see instead through eyes of compassion, the pattern of violence stops with us. We can then become proactive agents of real change.

The Choice is Yours

So compassion is not some bland, artificially sweetened tea that you drink while you whistle away the woes of the world. On the contrary, it's the strongest brew around. It demands a lot of us, perhaps more than we can manage in some moments.

To be crystal clear once again, love and compassion do not mean that you make yourself a doormat for people to walk all over, or that you fail to respond appropriately to the harmful actions of others. On the contrary, love *demands* an effective response. You may well choose not to interact with a particular person in order to protect yourself or others. You may well choose to vigorously condemn and actively oppose harmful actions. In fact, love will vastly strengthen your resolve to do so. The difference is that your own actions will be guided by understanding rather than reaction. *You will become a part of the solution rather than unwittingly adding to the problem.*

If suggestions to "love your enemies" rankle you or incite resistance, it may be helpful to remember again that we aren't talking about some kind of moral nicety or commandment. We're talking about an indispensable foundation for your own well being. In the wake of horrible violence or injustice, you may feel vast waves of pain and rage. That's only natural. Glossing over the world's evils certainly won't do. But eventually, love demands of each of us that we find within ourselves a greater power than hatred. There can be no other viable path. In time, with patience, hatred *can* soften, then melt, and the benefits we reap will be immeasurable.

For those who have personally suffered great abuse or injustice, Second-Order Compassion can be a challenge of tremendous, almost unbearable proportion. Though it is among the most heroic endeavors of the human heart, it begins in the simplicity of a fundamental choice – one that will shape the course of our lives forever. We either live as victims, holding fast to hatred and allowing ourselves to be driven by it. Or, we resolve to free ourselves, to break the cycle of reaction, to make ourselves agents of love and understanding in the world. This is the crossroads at which we stand. The stakes are tremendous, and the choice is ours alone to make.

A Native American grandfather was talking to his grandson

about how he felt about the tragedy on September 11.

He said, "I feel as if I have two wolves fighting in my heart.

One wolf is vengeful, angry, violent.

The other wolf is loving, forgiving, compassionate.

The grandson asked him: "Which wolf will win the fight in your heart."

The grandfather answered: "Whichever one I feed."

~Source unknown~

Chapter Six:
Overcoming Political Dogma

Political Economy and the Dangers of Dogma

When we care for others beyond our immediate circle, it quickly brings us into the realm of what was traditionally called *politics*. When people use the word politics these days, they're usually talking about something narrow or even corrupt. But its real meaning comes from *polis*, the "city-state" of ancient Greece. Politics in the true sense of the word is something that can lift us up. It has a powerful moral dimension in which we shape and share common life.

Although the political realm is by no means limited to economics, the dominant political ideologies of our time are largely economic in nature. When ideologies harden, they become dogma. And nowhere, with the possible exception of religion, does dogma rule the roost as much as it does in the ways that people think about politics and economics. It's a very dangerous phenomenon. As Nobel Peace Prize Nominee Thich Nhat Hanh says: "If you pick up a gun you can kill someone; if you pick up an ideology, you can kill millions."

If we're sincere in our desire to live our lives with love, we would do well to carefully check ourselves for any signs of infection with one of the various strains of political dogma. Whether or not we see ourselves as particularly political, we can at least keep our eyes open to the realities of our time and the world that surrounds us.

Whatever your political perspective – "right," "left," "middle," "not interested," "refuse to participate" or somehow "beyond it all," we're about to challenge what might be some cherished assumptions. We're not going to offer any "new and correct" ideology. We're just going to keep asking one key question that puts the fire under all our feet. Whatever the situation we face: *what would love do?*

Market Madness and the Dogma of Me: Psychological

We've already looked a bit at the "Ideology of Me." But economic markets can play a special role in taking the Ideology of Me to ever-higher, more dogmatic levels. They do so in at least two ways.

First, there's a powerful psychological process at work. If I'm a gazillionaire, and other people are starving, homeless or lack medical care, is there not a huge psychological incentive to find some good reason for the way things are? Especially if my wealth comes from anything that involves harm to others or environmental destruction, I'm faced with a pressing moral dilemma. To think that the situation is really wrong, that my wealth and privilege is somehow tied to other people's suffering would make for some really tough choices, wouldn't it?

If my affluence derives in any way from other people's suffering, and if love really matters to me, what choices am I left with? I can close my eyes and pretend not to see. I can close my heart, and decide that love doesn't really matter after all. I can try to glaze things over by saying "*I have to be realistic,*" "*That's just people's fate,*" or some such thing. Or, I can reach for whatever ideology I can to justify the situation.

What else am I to do? Conclude that I don't deserve my wealth, that I should give big chunks of it away, that I should change the industries and organizations that I'm involved with, or that the system itself should be overhauled to meet people's basic needs and protect the environment? Really, what are my alternatives?

Please understand: the point here isn't to convince anyone of a particular political perspective. If this all seems like liberal rhetoric, as I'm sure it will to some people, rest assured: in a few short passages, we'll skewer some seemingly liberal assumptions as well. The point is to be really honest — *ruthlessly honest* – about what motivates us. *Why* do we believe what we believe? That's what's most essential: instead of just clinging to our viewpoint, to be willing to look with courage and integrity at why we adopt the beliefs we adopt. Is our belief really just a purely rational calculation? Or is there a reason that we *want* to believe what we believe? Honestly facing this question is one of the most powerful steps we can take toward living a truly loving life, a life of honesty and integrity.

Market Madness and the Dogma of Me: Structural

In addition to psychological forces, there are actually forces inherent in the market economy itself that tend to push the Dogma of Me to extremes. It's not just people's personal psychology that sometimes makes it seem like love runs dry at the first sight of a dollar bill. The market can actually provide powerful incentives to do exactly the wrong thing.

If I can gain advantage over my competitors by scrimping on wages or health, safety, and environmental standards, doing so may seem like the only path to success, or even economic

survival. Because if I do the *right* thing – if I produce only benefi-
cial goods and services, pay people well, choose trading partners
who respect human rights, and adopt high environmental standards – I can actually put myself out of business. Someone else
with lower standards can win out by selling the same product
cheaper.

I'm also pushed to produce certain things rather than others.
Selling weapons to warlords in Africa, cigarettes to children in
Asia, and dumping the toxic waste from production into some
poor community in Mexico may be far more profitable than producing fresh vegetables for school lunch programs in Tennessee.

Of course, I may feel internally torn about all this. I may
genuinely care about other people. I may care about the kind of
world I leave behind to my children or grandchildren or great-
grandchildren. I may even care about what happens to other
people's children and grandchildren. It's unlikely that I truly *want*
to contribute to torture, disease, starvation, or rampant pollution. I may not even believe that the approach is sustainable for
my own business.

But in a competitive economy, I may feel tremendous pressure to show positive financial results *this quarter*. Without a law
that applies equally to me and everyone else, I'm often penalized
for doing the right thing, and pushed to do things that I'd never
choose to do face-to-face to another human being.

Granted, this is a very simplified scenario. But it is *the* basic
scenario, with variations, that plays itself out in a thousand different businesses and board rooms each day. The idea that the
invisible hand of economic markets will take care of everything
all by itself, with no moral or structural constraints, is destined

to leave behind nothing but a wasteland. It is an ideology that gets marketed as freedom, but it actually destroys true human freedom very quickly. It pushes people to do evil even when their hearts might tell them to do good. No dogmatic free market ideologue has ever been able to answer this, and none can, because it's built into the very structure of the market economy.

So we might ask ourselves in the midst of such a mess: *what would love, care, empathy, or even simple human decency do?*

The Dogma of We

The main response to the insanity of the aforementioned free-for-all has been to use the force of law to regulate economic markets. At its most extreme, this has involved attempts to violently wrest control of the entire economy by the apparatus of the state. That was the path chosen by Vladimir Lenin, and then Joseph Stalin, which resulted in one of the bloodiest genocides in all of human history. By some estimates, it resulted in roughly ten million deaths by forced famine and terror.

There are, of course, far more benign, beneficent approaches, such as the social democracies of Europe, especially the Nordic nations, which include a relatively vibrant private sector along with public control of essential enterprises like education and health care.

The extent to which the economy is privatized or state-owned and operated varies widely in Europe, Asia, Africa and the Americas. Even in the United States, Social Security, Medicare, Medicaid, and lower education are all publicly provided. This short book is not the place to explore all of the ideological variants, or all of the differences in actually existing nation-states. But as a general principle, the more that people seek to enforce centralized controls and constraints upon the economy, the more they run into at least three inherent problems:

First, controlling and planning economic life constrains risk-taking, creativity, and spontaneity.

Second, it distances the process of decision-making from the people whose lives are affected. Power is moved from individuals, families, and communities to centralized bureaucracies where those who supposedly know better dictate from afar. Law and public policy become increasingly complex, and often indecipherable to anyone but highly specialized "experts." And even the experts seem lost much of the time. So a bureaucrat in Washington DC decides what's best for a farmer in Omaha, a grocery store owner in Atlanta, a microchip maker in San Jose, or a factory worker in Detroit.

As people become increasingly disempowered and distanced from the decisions that shape their lives, they become less engaged, less civic-minded, and less trustful of the entire political process. Politics ceases to be an ethically rich, participatory process of shaping and sharing common life, and instead becomes a massive machine to arbitrate competing interests. "We the people" become too big and impersonal to really function as a "we" anymore. We become an increasingly faceless mass that's mainly swayed through manipulation. "Buy this toothpaste, this policy, this candidate," we're told, and it will benefit your pocketbook. Meanwhile, the real sponsors, motives, and impacts of public policies become more and more obscure. Instead of lifting us up and bringing out the best in us, politics starts to take us down by appealing to the lowest common denominator.

There's a third, closely related problem inherent in state controls on economic markets, and it sends us straight back to the pretzel example from my childhood (when the woman tried to bribe us with pretzels to clean up her yard). The natural human empathetic response (love) doesn't function very well under the use of bribery, threat, or force. If I'm required to do a lot of things, a part of me rebels, and I increasingly do only what I'm forced to do. If I'm bribed, I begin to do things just for the payoff. Subjected to too much command and control, my natural capacity for altruism starts to atrophy.

So the *Dogma of We* actually undermines the *true consciousness of we*, as people become increasingly distanced from the sources of power and from each other, increasingly "atomized" and disempowered. No liberal dogma has ever been able to adequately contend with these issues, because they're built right into the very impulse to control and command.

Again, my point isn't to convince anyone of a particular political belief. You may or may not agree with all the specifics I've laid out. My point is to encourage self-awareness and to invite you to bring a critical eye to *all* of the prevailing dogmas that you're likely to come across.

Ideology and Ego

As we begin to bring this kind of self-awareness to our belief systems, we start seeing why we may *want* to believe something, what consequences the belief holds for us. If, for example, I confront my own belief systems, I may find that I get something overt from a particular belief, such as a justification for holding onto money or power. Or, to return to an earlier theme, I may find that there's a more subtle motivation of *ego*, of how I define myself. This is especially important to recognize, because the entire cycle of human destructiveness is often fiercely fueled by the impulse to define ourselves *in opposition to something*.

For example, an Islamic Fundamentalist may define himself in opposition to what he sees as the modern moral decay of the West. Without the evil of the West, he would suffer a total identity crisis. Likewise, as an American, if I want to justify my own warlike impulses or institute rigid controls in my own society, the potential for fundamentalist terror can provide precisely what I need. These impulses are often unconscious, and calling them out would usually issue forth the most vehement denials from those involved. But if you look closely, you can see the process at work. The more identified we are with our views, the more we absolutely need our adversaries to continue just as they are, otherwise, *we as we know ourselves* would cease to exist.

To say it another way, the more we're stuck in our views, the more we depend on the very thing we oppose to give our life meaning, purpose, and clarity. That's why part of the right-wing libertarian free-marketer loves Karl Marx, and part of the left-wing liberal loves the abusive corporation. Or, to use an example that hits closer to home for some of us, there's a place in the heart of many environmentalists that absolutely *loves* climate change. While there may be a strong scientific basis for believing that human-induced climate change is real and destructive, there's also an emotional motivation for environmentalists to believe in it. It ups the stakes, intensifies the drama, proves the bigness of the cause, so that our mission in life is made clear and compelling. What most of us fail to see is how this kind of hidden motive hijacks us, how it taints our ability to act effectively, to act with love, and to bring about real change.

Lest there be any misunderstanding, overcoming this hidden motive does not mean that we shouldn't have any opinions, or that we should turn into indecisive mud puddles. What it means is simply that we can be more aware of our motives, of what's driving us. We can then choose to respond more effectively, with compassion instead of unnecessary hatred and division. We'll look more closely at this process in our last section *(The Greatest Love)*.

Admittedly, we've only scratched the surface of a number of important political questions. But we have other issues to get on to, so the deeper political explorations will have to wait for another book. However, there are a few crucial, related points that we need to explore, because they go right to the heart of our subject – of what it takes to truly live a life of love.

The Courage To Engage and Reflect

First, it's important to face the fact that there's no way to truly avoid the political realm. We're all political whether we want to be or not. The only question is whether we're conscious or unconscious about the process, whether we're awake or asleep at the wheel. Every day, we do things that have consequences to others beyond our immediate circle. And life beyond our immediate circle is affecting us right now, whether we're aware of it or not. Our well being, our freedom, the very substance of our lives is intimately intertwined with the lives of others in myriad ways that are sometimes seen and most often unseen.

But here's the great challenge. Because the broader world can often seem so harsh or overwhelming, it takes courage to engage with it. Exactly *how* to engage with it is different for each of us, but it generally means being at least minimally tuned in to what's happening in your own community as well as on a more global level. It means keeping an eye on things, reading at least some news – not to get overwhelmed by the magnitude and intensity of it all, but to glean what might be relevant for your life and the lives of those you love.

Effective political awareness is not a matter of passive spectatorship or glued-to-the-news obsession. It's really a process of intuitive listening. You listen to the rhythm of the world, and sense if there might be a moment that calls you to take some kind of action. The calling is different for each of us. Some of us are born to be ardent activists our entire lives. Others are hooked up to lead quieter lives.

But don't be too sure you know which category you fit into! It's all about the listening. Especially if you're someone who feels like your own situation and concerns are already overwhelming enough without worrying about the rest of the world, you may be surprised. It's often by picking our heads up and looking at things from a broader perspective that we remember what matters most, and find balance in our own lives. There may be some very personal lessons waiting for *you* out in that broader world.

Likewise, if you're someone who is constantly engaged in efforts to change the outward circumstances of the world but find it hard to take quiet time for yourself, you may receive great nourishment from solitude and simple appreciation of all that's good and right about life just as it is. When you then return to action, you may find that you're more effective, and that it's easier to act out of joy and love rather than guilt or compulsion. Just as it takes courage to engage in the world, so it can also take a kind of courage to face oneself, to be with life as it is.

The Joy of Service

When we're called by love to take part in something larger than ourselves, it can vastly enrich and ennoble our lives. It can bring a kind of happiness that purely personal success rarely if ever rivals. When he was running for President of the United States, John McCain said "serve a cause greater than self-interest, and you will know a happiness far more sublime than the fleeting pleasure of fame and fortune."

Although I confess I didn't vote for Senator McCain, there were aspects of his character that I deeply respected. (Does that put me in a small minority, to disagree with a presidential candidate and still respect him?) It was also John McCain who defined patriotism as "countless acts of love, kindness and courage that have no witness or heraldry and are especially commendable because they are unrecorded."

The point is this: whatever may call to you, don't be afraid to step outside your comfort zone to positively affect someone else's life, to touch the world in new ways. There's a part of all of us that longs for that. We need only listen for it, and to overcome the voices (our own or others') that tell us we're powerless. Even now, as you read these words, you may be far more powerful than you can possibly imagine.

The Butterfly Effect and the Oil Spill

Here's one very factual way to understand why you may be more powerful than you suspect.

In 1961, MIT Professor Edward Lorenz was using a numerical computer model to rerun a weather prediction. As a shortcut, he entered the decimal .506 instead of entering the full .506127. Much to his surprise, this one small variation totally changed the resulting weather scenario. The experience informed Lorenz's theoretical models, and a fellow meteorologist remarked that if the Lorenz's theory was correct, "one flap of a seagull's wings could change the course of weather forever."

Lorenz later took to using the example of a butterfly. His 1972 address to the American Association for the Advancement of Science was titled *Does the flap of a butterfly's wings in Brazil set off a tornado in Texas?* The flapping wing represents a small change in the initial condition of a system, which causes a chain of events leading to large-scale alterations. And so, the term *Butterfly Effect* was born.

The principle of the Butterfly Effect has important implications not only for the natural sciences, but also for the social sciences, and even for how we perceive the events of daily life. I happen to be writing this passage shortly after the massive British Petroleum oil spill in the Gulf of Mexico. The spill has rightly been described as a major disaster. In addition to taking the lives of eleven workers and injuring seventeen, the spill will have long-lasting impacts on the economy and the culture of the region, as well as potentially catastrophic impacts on the ecosystems of the Gulf. Entire ways of life going back generations will be lost, as will much of the richness and diversity of numerous marine ecosystems, including those of eight national parks.

One of the most remarkable things about the BP Spill is that it could likely have been avoided at very minimal cost. The House Energy and Finance committee concluded that BP "ignored continuous warnings and abnormalities" regarding the possibility of a catastrophic spill. But BP wanted to avoid paying the $500,000 rental fee for the rig that it was trying to close down. (This from a company that was making sixty-three million dollars *per day* in *profits*.)

Now, the easy, popular thing to do is simply to blame BP for the "evilness" of its actions. But if you think about it, no one would ever have knowingly made the decision to unleash the explosion and resulting disaster. On the contrary, someone in the chain of command made a decision to overlook what were hopefully small abnormalities and risks, and perhaps save the company a couple million dollars. It was just a small decision to cut corners, to look the other way, to rush the process, to ignore the reality, to act irresponsibly based on short-term interests. Imagine their shock as they witnessed their tiny misstep take the lives of eleven people, kill untold numbers of sea animals, spew over two-hundred million gallons of oil, wipe out a hundred billion dollars of their company's value, and unleash one of the largest environmental disasters in history.

But here's the message to take away from this event. Earlier, we quoted John McCain. This time the insight comes from the other side of the political spectrum, from Van Jones, the author of *The Green-Collar Economy*, who resigned from the Obama Adminstration after repeated attacks from Fox News. Jones says of the BP spill:

*"A very tiny, tiny act based on greed created a non-linear massively bad outcome.... But in a symmetrical, rational, beautiful universe, that means: if a small act based on greed can create a non-linear, horrific outcome... then small acts based on love can create non-linear, unbelievably beautiful outcomes. Just like that person at BP when he or she made that small cheat based on greed, had no idea how much harm he or she was going to do, **you** have no idea how much good you are going to do, how much good you are capable of."*

The key, says Jones, is to stay focused on love.

"But love ain't easy... when it gets harder to love, love harder."

I can think of no wiser counsel for the realm of politics – or for religion, the subject to which we now turn.

Chapter Seven:
Overcoming Religious Dogma

Child's Eyes

There's a story my mother loves to tell about a cross-country road trip that my family took one summer when we were still living on the East Coast. Driving through the Dakotas on our way to California, my parents and older siblings became immersed in a heated debate about the existence of God.

My father (an accomplished biochemist) and my teenage brother and sister were all taking the position that we should only believe something if it can be rationally proven. My mother, on the other hand, insisted that she believed in God as a matter of faith, regardless of what anyone else said or any logic that they might present.

The argument had been going on for nearly an hour, during which time I'd been sitting quietly, gazing at the orange glow that the setting sun was painting on the horizon. (As a hyperactive seven-year-old, it was highly unusual for me to sit quietly for sixty seconds, let alone sixty minutes.) Finally, I spoke up: *"Dad?"* *"Yes, Jeff?"* *"How can you look at that sunset and say you don't believe in God?"* And as my mother loves to tell the story, "that shut them all up. The argument was over."

The Nature of Religious Dogma

I retell this story to help make clear at the outset of this chapter that the criticism of religious dogma that follows is in no way meant as a categorical rejection of religion *per se*. I've always personally embraced what might be considered a religious or spiritual worldview — a sense that some larger order of things is at work in the universe.

I also sympathize with the dilemma that many religious people face when trying to communicate their faith. It's natural that we should want to share something that we feel has a profoundly positive impact on our lives, and it's not always easy to know the best way to do that. Before jumping on any anti-religious bandwagon, I would even go so far as to suggest that one of today's most dogmatic religious ideologies is what might be called *"Anti-Religion"* or *"Scientific Fundamentalism"* — a subject that we'll touch on near the end of the chapter.

Nevertheless, for all of these caveats, the damage that religious dogma can do is tremendous. Whether we look at the bloodshed that has ensued in the course of religious conquest, the cruelty and abuses carried out by religious leaders, or the looming threats of terrorism and reprisal that cast a pall over global events in our time, history is replete with instances when religious doctrine has been at the epicenter of human violence and vitriol. Pick up an ideology and you can kill millions. Pick up a religious ideology and you can kill millions convinced that you are doing God's will.

The Doctrine of Reward and Punishment

Religious dogma can be about a lot of different things, but it often begins with doctrines of reward and punishment. If you're good, you go to heaven or reap the benefits of your positive karma. If you're bad (which all too often means if you don't believe exactly what *we* do) then you face the prospect of eternal damnation.

These systems of reward and punishment may serve to enforce a certain morality upon us, but they also have the effect of leading away and astray from love. That's not to say that we should never reward or punish anyone. It just means that whenever we do, we're making an important compromise that comes at a cost. We're taking a step down and away from a true ethic of love.

Bribing and threatening people appeals to their selfishness and fear. Seeking to uplift or inspire them appeals to their capacity for love. These forces pull at the human heart from opposite sides and cannot simultaneously prevail.

The Afterlife and the Mind of God

Where principles of religious reward and punishment are usually most clearly spelled out is in various doctrines about an afterlife. I can't claim to know with certainty what happens after the death of the body, but I've surely heard from many who do claim to know, often with remarkable specificity. Such claims come from people of various religious faiths, but living in the United States I mainly hear them from prominent Christian religious figures.

I once saw a wealthy televangelist say that he died for a day and went to heaven. When he got there, it was a city filled with condominiums and swimming pools. Thousands of followers watched in amazement to witness this gospel truth and to donate large sums of their hard earned cash so that the message could be spread far and wide.

Far less amusing in my mind are the pronouncements of those who claim to read God's precise moral judgments in earthly events. These self-proclaimed prophets almost seem to delight in human suffering as they transmit the Lord's personal messages that hurricanes, earthquakes and tsunamis are punishment for the evils of homosexuality, false religious beliefs, and other supposed sins. Perhaps it would be easier to digest their sermons had I never read what Jesus is reported to have said. But I have, and it seems clear that love was a central theme.

What Jesus Meant

The ideological starting point for many fundamentalists is the biblical passage that reads "I am the truth the way and the light and only through me shall you enter the Kingdom of Heaven." Exactly what Jesus meant by this statement is, of course, open to broad interpretation. In fact, I wonder if it isn't a classic example of human arrogance – the very kind that the bible so often cautions against – that we would presume to know with absolute certainty what Jesus intended two-thousand years ago, based on what was written down many years later.

If we have any interest in knowing anything of value about Jesus at all, it would seem to me we might best begin by seeking to love as he loved. If Jesus were alive in the flesh today, I expect he would see religious fundamentalism as one of his greatest adversaries. Fundamentalism is, I believe, the farthest from Jesus in spirit even as it may proclaim itself the closest in word. It averts the humbling challenge of living with an open heart by securing for itself the false certainty of living with a closed mind.

But The Good Book Says

And what if we do take the Bible to be the timeless, literal, perfected expression of God's truth and will? This is what Professor James Kaufmann endeavored to do in an open letter to radio host Dr. Laura Schlesinger after Schlesinger insisted that homosexuality can never be condoned because it's an abomination according to Leviticus 18:22.

The following is Kaufmann's letter as posted on the Internet. While the tone of the letter is intensely acerbic, it presents a very real challenge to any of us who would cite scripture to substantiate our views, or especially to condemn others.

Dear Dr. Laura:

1. *Leviticus 25:44 states that I may possess slaves, both male and female, provided they are from neighboring nations. A friend of mine claims that this applies to Mexicans, but not Canadians. Can you clarify? Why can't I own Canadians?*

2. *I would like to sell my daughter into slavery, as sanctioned in Exodus 21:7. In this day and age, what do you think would be a fair price for her?*

3. *I know that I am allowed no contact with a woman while she is in her period of Menstrual uncleanliness - Lev.15: 19-24. The problem is how do I tell? I have tried asking, but most women take offense.*

4. *When I burn a bull on the altar as a sacrifice, I know it creates a pleasing odor for the Lord - Lev.1:9. The problem is my neighbors. They claim the odor is not pleasing to them. Should I smite them?*

5. *I have a neighbor who insists on working on the Sabbath. Exodus 35:2 clearly states he should be put to death. Am I morally obligated to kill him myself, or should I ask the police to do it?*

6. *A friend of mine feels that even though eating shellfish is an abomination, Lev. 11:10, it is a lesser abomination than homosexuality. I don't agree. Can you settle this? Are there 'degrees' of abomination?*

7. *Lev. 21:20 states that I may not approach the altar of God if I have a defect in my sight. I have to admit that I wear reading glasses. Does my vision have to be 20/20, or is there some wiggle-room here?*

8. *Most of my male friends get their hair trimmed, including the hair around their temples, even though this is expressly forbidden by Lev. 19:27. How should they die?*

9. *I know from Lev. 11:6-8 that touching the skin of a dead pig makes me unclean, but may I still play football if I wear gloves?*

10. *My uncle has a farm. He violates Lev.19:19 by planting two different crops in the same field, as does his wife by wearing garments made of two different kinds of thread (cotton/polyester blend). He also tends to curse and blaspheme a lot. Is it really necessary that we go to all the trouble of getting the whole town together to stone them? Lev.24:10-16. Couldn't we just burn them to death at a private family affair, like we do with people who sleep with their in-laws? (Lev. 20:14) I know you have studied these things extensively and thus enjoy considerable expertise in such matters, so I'm confident you can help. Thank you again for reminding us that God's word is eternal and unchanging.*

Your adoring fan.
James M. Kauffman, Ed.D. Professor Emeritus,
Dept. Of Curriculum, Instruction, and Special Education
University of Virginia
PS (It would be a damn shame if we couldn't own a Canadian)

Be Your Own Authority

Again, though the tone of Kauffman's letter is sarcastic, the challenge that it presents is very real. If we cite religious authority to justify our views, what *do* we do with endorsements of slavery and the like? If, on the other hand, we take religious scripture to be profound but nevertheless time-bound and humanly mediated, then we must acknowledge that our own capacity for reason, faith and intuition must play a key role in determining the life path that we choose, either individually or collectively.

To be a bit more bold: perhaps if we want to discover what Jesus, Moses, Mohammed, Buddha, or any other religious figure was talking about, we have to awaken to what they awakened to. The danger of that, of course, is that it threatens to take the "middlemen" out of the equation. The "middlemen" – the priests, ministers, rabbis, roshis and lamas – cease to be mere middlemen, and become truly helpful when they help us get in touch with our own innate wisdom. Instead of setting themselves up as infallible mediators between us and God, they become true guides who help support us each in following our own path.

In other words, the point is not to reject all authority, but rather to anchor authority in a spirit of freedom and open inquiry. Many of history's greatest contributions have come from those who are inspired by deep faith, and whose faith and teachings are rooted in love and tolerance rather than doctrinal division. The spirit of their leadership is open and egalitarian, and the authority with which they speak is earned rather than assigned.

Children of God

If we look closely, we can actually find this open, egalitarian spirit showing up in some rather surprising places. Consider for example *The Lord's Prayer,* perhaps the most popular in all of Christianity. "Our Father which art in heaven..." The point is made self-evident right there. The Lord's Prayer does not merely say "Jesus' Father which art in heaven. It says "Our Father," meaning that *you* are the daughter or son of God as much as anyone. And while Jesus may have brought a new beginning, you *too* bring a new beginning in each moment that you are truly awake to life. The sacredness of life did not end two thousand years ago, nor did the possibility of human renewal.

Of course, if you aren't religiously oriented, this is less a personal exploration than an inquiry into some extremely influential belief systems that have done much to shape the world as we know it. Either way, let's take the inquiry a step farther: Is it possible that the Lord's Prayer is itself ready for a new beginning? What if the Prayer were recited *"Our Mother-Father"* (as I have heard it recited in some congregations?) Does it really make sense to confine our concept of the Infinite to a single gender? Is the fact that women have been subjugated for millennia an excuse for clinging to a tradition that would cut them right out of creation? Surely as men we can be expected to have grown secure enough in our masculinity that we can at last acknowledge women as an integral part of creation, of all that is good, divine and essential, can we not?

Karma Dogma

At this point, it's important to acknowledge that the spirit of openness and respect for diversity that we've called forth in relation to the Judeo-Christian tradition applies equally to other traditions as well. In the case of Islam, many of the points that have been made can easily be extrapolated, and the contrast between the demands of dogma and those of love may only seem more extreme.

Of the other major religious traditions, certain Asian systems (Hinduism, Buddhism, and Taoism for example) present their own special doctrinal challenges. Alas, it seems that there can sometimes be a tendency among Westerners who are immersed in Asian spirituality to fancy ourselves less primitive or superstitious than those who adhere to Jewish, Christian, or Muslim faiths. Admittedly, there are certain Asian spiritual traditions that tend to have a logical, analytical flavor that may seem consistent with a modern scientific worldview. At least they seem to contrast favorably with simplistic Sunday school versions of theism that picture God as an old man in a white beard who sits on a cloud and creates the world in a week.

But that doesn't necessarily mean that the Eastern traditions are immune to superstition, dogma, or irrationality. Take the doctrine of karma, for example.

On one hand, karma can be a sensible insight into the relationship between cause and effect. Certain actions tend to produce certain effects, and wisdom involves the ability to discern the effects that various actions are likely to bring about. On the other hand, the teachings of karma can easily become another form of dogma – "Karma Dogma" if you will.

Karma Dogma says that everything you experience in your life comes from the morality or immorality of your past deeds. You got robbed because you robbed someone else in a past lifetime, or some such thing. It's important to recognize that many of these doctrines were propagated millennia ago by highly privileged religious hierarchies. That doesn't mean that we should necessarily reject them out of hand. But perhaps we can have the courage to at least ask a few questions.

For the way that we approach these issues goes straight back to the question of whether the ethic of our lives shall fundamentally be made of love, or of fear. It is a critically important question that reaches into every aspect of life, from politics, religion and commerce, to childrearing and our closest personal relationships.

Karma Questions

Here are four questions to ask anyone who claims to know how karma works, and who draws a specific correlation between your past deeds and your present experience:

First, how do you know? It's a really important question: how can you or anyone possibly know? If this question cannot be answered convincingly, then the whole ideology is, at a minimum, thrown into question.

Second, to use one tangible example, if the sole or even the main reason someone gets robbed is their own karmic inheritance, then if I rob you, aren't I just bringing about the fulfillment of your own karma?

Third, if we're actually all connected and don't exist as totally discreet, isolated egos, then does it ever make sense to talk about a single cause for anything that happens? The core insight of the Asian traditions is that all things are interrelated. Would it not then make more sense to see actions and results as part of a vast interrelated web that includes both personal and social responsibility?

Fourth, on a practical level, what's the effect of telling a woman who has been raped or had a family member murdered that it's simply her karma? Why preach, why impose, why even hypothesize what we do not and cannot know?

Love Is The Greatest Reward

The bottom line is this: There's nothing wrong with believing in karma or not believing in karma. But love has no need for ideology. To those who would cling to Buddhist, Hindu, or Taoist doctrines of reward and punishment, I would simply offer what I see at the core of each of those traditions: *that love is its own reward.* My guess is that religious figures from Moses to Jesus to Buddha to Mohammed all knew that perfectly well, and then some followers went badly astray. But that's just my educated guess, and can be little more. I can't know with certainty what they said or meant, and I question whether anyone else can either.

Even more importantly, whatever truth any prophet or religious figure experienced – if it really is true, lasting, and relevant – is right here and now for each of us to experience. This not only suggests a different view of religious experience and authority. It actually points to an alternate way of perceiving the meaning of eternity itself.

Religion often conceives of eternity as an afterlife in which we reap the consequences of what we've sown in this life. Alternatively, instead of seeing eternity as somewhere we go after we die, it's also possible to see it as something we awaken to right here and now. The "power of now" as it has delightfully been called, is not merely an idea of the present that exists in the gap between the past and the future. It is the reality that we experience without the perceptual filters with which we habitually divide life into segments of space and time. It is "the eternal present" and is often most easily perceived in the quiet spaces between our thoughts.

And if all this seems too heady, no matter. The point here isn't to adopt a new and better doctrine. It is to bring down whatever conceptual and emotional barriers may be standing in the way of our fully experiencing and expressing love right here and now in the midst of life.

Scientific Fundamentalism

As promised, the last form of religious dogma that we'll touch upon is one that considers itself utterly rational and free of all religious mythology. It is sometimes called *Scientism;* I'll refer to it here as *Scientific Fundamentalism.*

In essence, Scientific Fundamentalism categorically rejects all forms of religion, and assumes that it knows a great many things about which it actually knows very little. Like other forms of dogma, Scientific Fundamentalism is a powerful obstacle to love, to the "reasons of the heart" which narrow calculating reason can never comprehend. Just as I have suggested that militant and fundamentalist Christians are farthest from the spirit of Jesus' teaching, so I believe that those who are dogmatically scientific are farthest from the true spirit of science. This also happens to be the view of many of the world's greatest scientists.

Einstein, for example, spoke of the "cosmic religious feeling" which he considered the "strongest and noblest motive for scientific research." Schroedinger proclaimed the gross deficiency of the conventional "scientific picture of the real world," which he said is "ghastly silent about all and sundry that is really near to our heart." "It knows nothing," Schroedinger insisted, about "beautiful and ugly, good or bad, God and eternity." Likewise, Werner Heisenberg excoriated those who would reduce human concern to that which can be proven, measured, or rationally delineated and articulated. "Can anyone conceive of a more pointless philosophy" asked Heisenberg, "seeing that what we can say clearly amounts to next to nothing?"

When science fancies itself farther along than it actually is, it quickly loses its way. I wholeheartedly concur with the aforementioned physicists that its true way is actually not separate from matters of the spirit. Perhaps there will come a day when we finally transcend many of the longstanding divisions between the scientific and religious worldviews, when we will attain a greater wholeness and a higher synthesis. Though pure conjecture, the following are a few example of what a higher synthesis might look like.

Perhaps a day will come when we accept evolution without requiring that it be considered "blind." Perhaps we will one day accept the Big Bang as the origin of this unfolding universe as we know it, without believing that "nothing" actually went "bang," or that all of existence actually "began" at that particular moment. Perhaps we'll eventually conclude that our very search for a "beginning" of the universe is actually faulty, that presupposing a beginning in time is a fundamental error in logic, and that both science and religion have often been on the wrong track, debating like two people arguing how far the flat earth extends in each direction before you fall off the edge.

Again, all of this is mere conjecture, though it can be fun to think about. And all of it would be beyond our subject matter, except for one thing: Love yearns for something larger than that which meets the eye. Call it *God*, call it *Source*, call it *Life*, call it *Universe* — call it whatever you like and believe about it whatever you will. But there is a part of us that longs for wholeness, and that part can never be completely or lastingly filled by the people, places and things we may reach to. Only the whole can bring wholeness. While scientific and religious dogma may have misled us in their attempts to help us find our way, a greater love is possible in our lives.

Chapter Eight:
Your Greatest Love

Your Relationship With Life

We've been looking at love from various angles, turning it like a crystal in the light to better perceive its many hues and patterns. It's time now to ask a simple but very important question:

Do you truly love life?

It's the kind of question that provokes a variety of initial responses. You might answer automatically: "of course I love life, what are you talking about?" You might break straight for the spiritual or poetic: "life is a precious gift, a wonder, a blessing." Maybe you reflect a bit, and decide that what you actually love are *parts* of life. You love chocolate, sunsets, sports, time with friends, or curling up with a good book. You don't like mean people, traffic jams, pollution, warfare, or calls from telemarketers. Perhaps you conclude that your relationship to life actually depends on your state of mind – you love life when you relate to it with acceptance and gratitude, and you don't when you're reactive.

Instead of answering with whatever first comes to mind, you can also use the question to cut deeper, to look more closely at how you actually *experience* life. We often view our lives through powerful mental and emotional filters that tend to go completely unnoticed. When we begin to recognize these filters, we can actually start seeing beyond them, and the possibilities of love grow larger in our lives. Let's flesh out what this means with a couple of examples.

Analogy of the Loving Parent

The following are two hypothetical scenarios that can serve as analogies for the larger question of how you relate to life as a whole. The first scenario is how you might relate to a child.

Let's say you have a thirteen-year old son named Michael. Michael's just finishing junior high and he's had a rough year. His grades have dropped, he got into a couple of fights, and he was suspended from school for a week. Michael is often a great kid. He's athletic, can be very helpful when you least expect it, and he's terrifically funny. Sometimes you can't believe the wonderful, quirky things that come out of his mouth.

But Michael also gets bored easily, and he can have a terrible temper. A few months ago, he got mad when you told him to clean his room for the umpteenth time, and before his tantrum was done he had smashed his bedroom window. At school, even the smallest provocation can infuriate him and goad him to throw a punch. Last summer, he and a couple friends were caught torturing a frog. At the time, he thought it was terrifically funny, but you were extremely taken aback and disappointed in him. It's been very stressful to watch your son act out his aggression over the past year, and to try to figure out how to deal with him.

Now, suppose someone comes and asks you if you love Michael. You might answer in any number of ways. You might say something like "of course, he's my son." You might say "yes, I love Michael very much; he's had problems lately, but he's basically a good kid." What you probably won't say is "yes, my son Michael is an angel. He never does anything wrong." What you also probably won't say, is "Well, I love him when he's good, and I hate him when he's bad." That might not be far from the way you feel at times, but it's unlikely you'd answer quite that way. You might say something like "well, I don't always like him, but I always love him."

That last answer is actually a very interesting one. *"I don't always like him, but I always love him."* If someone asks what you mean by that, you might say something like "Michael sometimes acts in really lousy ways that I don't understand, but I know him at his core, and I know that he's basically a good person." You might even tell a story to explain what you mean… "Do you know, at swim camp one year, Michael was friends with Jason, the smallest kid in the camp. A couple big kids ganged up on Jason and threw his lunch in the lake. Michael called Jason over and gave him his whole lunch; he said he wasn't hungry. Michael never mentioned a word about it. Jason's Mom told me later."

So, as a loving parent, you don't live in denial about your son as though he were a perfect angel. And you don't make your love dependent upon how he does from one day to the next. You're steadier than that. There may be parts of Michael that you're not crazy about, parts that you're hoping will change, and maybe even some parts that you don't expect ever will. But Michael isn't a combination plate that you order at a restaurant. You don't get to pick and choose. You remember the good that he's capable of, and *you love him as a whole person, despite his faults.*

Analogy of the Loving Spouse

Here's another type of scenario you might run into. Let's say you're at a wedding and you happen to sit next to an elderly couple, Frank and Louise. The three of you chat for a while, then Frank gets up to get some cake, and you and Louise get to talking:

"Louise, tell me, what's it been like going through life with Frank all these years?"

"Frank? Oh, what a pain in the butt! Every afternoon, the bum watches TV and falls asleep and snores like a horse for two hours. I can barely hear myself think he snores so loud! Let me tell you, sometimes, the things I have to put up with."

She keeps going on, so you finally interject:

"So do you love him?"

"Do I love him? Frank? (Big smile) Let me tell you about Frank... When we were younger, we went for a long walk in the snow one time. I must have dropped my scarf someplace along the way. Do you know, Frank walked back over a mile in the snow in the dark that night just to find that old thing? It was so threadbare, you could barely even call it a scarf anymore. But my daughter gave me that scarf for my birthday one year when our son was overseas. That was the year that my father was really sick (beginning of elaborate half-hour story ...)

So Louise complains about Frank, and maybe she could learn to complain less. But she loves him, and though she never answers the question directly, her face immediately lights up when you ask her about her love for her husband. She knows Frank's faults, and all the little things that drive her nuts. But she loves "her Frank," as she sometimes calls him, and the two of them have stood by each other through thick and thin.

Bargaining and Bickering

In both of these examples, loving the other person takes commitment. As a parent, you don't get to select the characteristics of your child. As a husband or wife, you don't get to pick and choose which qualities of your spouse to keep and which to send back. You do your best to love the person as a whole, and you make an important commitment to stop seeking for an ideal. Your love is an act of devotion, an inner movement of the heart that gives up seeking and surrenders itself to the relationship, come what may.

Of course, it's possible that things may change and become intolerable, in which case you might ultimately separate or divorce. It's important that that option exists. But it's not something you would decide lightly. If you do stay together happily, it probably means that you've learned to love each other just as you are, even though you may not – even though you *will* not – like everything about each other.

Specifics aside, these two scenarios are really meant to point to something larger about our relationship with life itself. There's a sense in which many of us are still bargaining and bickering with life, trying to make it be something it isn't. We may spend tremendous energy trying to pick and choose and control life's outcomes. But somehow, life just doesn't seem to be the way it should be. Either *my life* isn't as it should be, so I need to keep chasing after various sources of fulfillment. Or, *the world* isn't as it should be – just look at all the poverty and warfare and pollution, and you can see how messed up everything is.

If we get caught in this pattern, we might pin our hopes on a better future. Or, we may despair that things will never get better. Either way, there's a sense in which our love for life has become very conditional and limited. We're like a fickle lover who's only satisfied for brief moments when we aren't acting, as Shaw said, like "a feverish, selfish little clod of ailments and grievances, complaining that the world will not devote itself to making (us) happy." Eventually, our relationship to life starts to resemble some miserably unhappy couple who stays together just because they don't know what else to do. We're not ready to end our own life (the only way to really get a divorce from life). That would be too drastic. But neither are we ready to accept life the way it is.

Thankfully, there is another way, a way that brings far greater love and fulfillment.

A Dialogue With Life

A number of years ago, I went through an especially challenging time – a "dark night of the soul" you could say. A strange turning point came one evening when I started to have what might be called a dialogue with Life. I could just as easily call it a dialogue with God, but I've learned that turns off some non-religious folks, so I'll just call it a dialogue with Life. The dialogue went something like this…

I said to Life: "I want a world where people are treated with respect and kindness instead of hatred and violence, where people are truly free."

Life said "I *gave* you the desire for people's well being. Every single longing that you ever feel in your heart, *I* placed there."

I said "I want a world where the air and water are clean, where the beauty of life is preserved and not destroyed."

Life said "I set the earth itself spinning in the sky. I created every life form you can ever see or know about. Each planet, each star, and every last speck of space, I alone created, and will endlessly destroy and recreate at will.

I said to Life: "I want a fulfilling romantic relationship." Life said "I *made* everyone you'll ever meet. They're all nothing more than brief reflections of me."

I said to Life: "I want to make some meaningful contribution in the world. I want to help people in some significant way." Life said "I gave you the desire to serve. Your greatest way of serving is simply to make yourself available to me."

And so our dialogue went on, until something in me shifted. I could call it acceptance or surrender, but that would really be too nice. To tell the truth, it felt more like a kind of defeat, or even death. Something in me was silenced that evening, and it changed my relationship to life. At first the change felt dramatic. Over time it seemed very subtle, but also very steady. I wrote about this experience in detail in *Living Joy*, so I won't go on here. The important point is that I ultimately came to realize that I had always been subtly at war with life. I *thought* I loved life, and in the end I did. But up until then, a lot of what I really loved was *my idea* of life instead of life as it really is.

Your Love Affair With Life

If you ask people what their very *greatest* love is, many will say their child or children, their spouse, or their family. Some will say laughter, or time in nature, or some other special activity. What I came to realize during that evening of dialogue was that my very greatest love is *life itself*. All the people, places and activities that I love – even those I love very deeply – are really reflections of my one primary love for life.

I realize that may sound abstract or insignificant, but it's actually a big shift. It involves seeing in ways that are very different than most of us are conditioned to see. It also involves falling very deeply in love with life – you could even say *committing* to life (even though you may not formally exchange vows or throw a party with cake and champagne).

Here are a few ways that I'd describe the experience if you were about to go through it. Of course, you may experience it differently; I just want to convey the essential meaning that I draw from it and leave it for you to see what might resonate:

- When you really fall in love with life, it means that you come to love the *whole* of life more than any one part, the *source* more than any particular manifestation. It's like you've lived your entire life transfixed by certain leaves and flowers on a tree, and you suddenly find yourself enamored with the tree itself.

- You see the unity of life – not just as an idea; you actually begin to sense life moving as one undivided whole that expresses itself in myriad ways.

- You turn your gaze from the fleeting fragments of existence, however beautiful they may be, to that which is lasting and essential. A certain restfulness begins to set in — even in the midst of busyness, even in the midst of changing moods and circumstances.

- You're acutely aware of your own mortality and that of everyone you know, and at the same time, you feel more and more deeply connected to that which will remain after you're gone. You see that each of us is like a wave on the ocean — a beautiful and unique expression — but that the ocean is one great, undivided body of water that merely changes appearances. You become increasingly identified with the water instead of just the wave.

- Similarly, you may see each person and event as a container that Life molds itself into for a brief moment. Even as you may love your spouse or child or friend, you are intimately, sensitively in touch with their fleeting nature.

- Because you know that each time you see someone may be your last, you're naturally more fully present for the people in your life.

A Great Awakening

The nature of love is that it softens one's boundaries, one's sense of self. When you love life very deeply, when you give yourself to life with devotion, you can start to feel very permeable and transparent, like you're a clear, open space through which life expresses itself. At times, your sense of separation can vanish entirely, and your identification with the whole of life becomes total. This can actually be a very dramatic awakening, a dramatic shift in perception, as though you've been looking at life through a small window your entire life, and suddenly you're seeing life directly. (We could even say you're looking *from* life directly, which is actually closer to the experience, but can be harder to grasp.)

The real shift, though, the shift that makes a lasting difference, isn't this dramatic epiphany. It's a more subtle movement of the heart that can be experienced at any time. The part of us that's so often at odds with life, battling for our gratification and our particular place in the world, *just lets go*. It's as though you've been rooting for your own "team" in your contest with life, and you suddenly switch teams and take life's side. (As someone once said, "in the battle between you and life, bet on life.")

"Taking life's side" means that you emotionally say *yes* to life as it is. It isn't that you suddenly love everything that happens. You don't necessarily "love" breaking your leg or getting pneumonia. You don't love genocide, torture, and every other horrible thing that happens in the world. But your love for life itself remains unshakeable even in the midst of all that's difficult. Your "yes" isn't a matter of personal agreement, as though life somehow needs you to agree. It's a matter of acceptance and openness to that which is.

Taken By Love

When I was a kid, my Mom used to serve a kind of tea called "Constant Comment." That's actually how a lot of our minds operate: we're constantly commenting on what we like and don't like, what we agree with and don't agree with, what we're for and against, and so on. We sometimes seem more in love with our running commentary than we are with life itself. Of course, I'm generalizing here; maybe you can only relate to a tiny sliver of this. But when we talked about ego earlier, about the tendency to separate ourselves out, this is its fuel – our constant mental chatter about our preferences and beliefs.

The alternative to separation and being driven by mental chatter isn't that we somehow stop having any thoughts, preferences or beliefs whatsoever. (Good luck with that if you try.) The alternative is loving acceptance. As you rest more in love and acceptance of things as they unfold, you stop caring so terribly much about whatever thought or feeling happens to be passing through you at the moment. In particular, you cease being run by the sense that life is a problem to be fixed. We can call this acceptance, love of what is, or even surrender. It can bring a deep sense of peace and well being. It's extremely important, though, not to confuse it with passivity or fatalism.

People often wonder: "if I accept life just as it is, won't I turn into a mud puddle incapable of doing anything at all? Won't I just sit around contemplating my navel or eating ice cream all day? Why would I ever take action to change things if I accepted them as they are?

The answer is: because it is your very nature to love. You can trust that just the way that you trust your body's ability to take your next breath without your having to do a whole lot about it. When you're open and receptive to life, love acts through you spontaneously, like water passing through an open channel. You love the same way that you breathe, or that you adjust your pillow at night when you sleep. There's no need for willful struggle, a rigid sense of duty, or dramas about the eternal battle between good and evil. You simply give yourself to love, and love takes you where it will, like a great and timeless stream.

If you really give yourself to that larger stream, there's no telling where it will take you. But you'll be lucky to ride its currents wherever they may lead. For though it can never be owned, love remains the single greatest gift that life has to offer. Please enjoy it and pass it along.

Further Resources

The Gift of Love is part of a larger body work advanced by the Human Fulfillment Institute (www.humanfulfillment.org). The Human Fulfillment Institute is a collaborative leadership group focused on the long-term effectiveness and fulfillment of organizations and individuals. We offer coaching, consulting, and a series of unique, interactive online courses that help bring about positive, lasting change.

The following courses are currently available at our online interactive practice center, called *Renewal Space* (www.renewalspace.net):

- Optimal Self-Care
- The Interactive Awareness Core Course
- Stress-Free Productivity
- Defeating Overeating
- Relationship Renewal
- Financial Freedom
- Finding True Love and Intimacy

Planned courses for the near future include:

- Everyday Soul-Care for the Busy Professional
- Training Your Boss: Mastering Communication within Teams and Organizations

Additional courses may include subject areas such as conscious parenting, effectiveness in social change organizations, vision and adaptation in green industry, and other topical focus areas. We frequently post free audio downloads and other materials.

If you or your organization are interested in coaching or consulting, please feel free to contact us at coaching@human-fulfillment.org

About The Author

Jeffrey David Ringold is Founder and Director of the Human Fulfillment Institute. A compelling speaker, life coach, and organizational consultant, Jeffrey is also the Founder, Publisher and Editor-In-Chief of *Renewal Space*, the interactive online practice center of the Human Fulfillment Institute. With an extensive background in personal growth, public policy, mediation and advocacy, Jeffrey's interests include a broad range of topics related to human leadership and fulfillment. Jeffrey has authored several online courses, including *Optimal Self-Care*, the *Interactive Awareness Core Course, Stress-Free Productivity and Fulfillment, Financial Freedom, and Finding True Love and Intimacy*. In addition to *The Gift of Love*, Jeffrey is the author of *Living Joy: A Practical Companion for the Well-Lived Life*.

Made in the USA
Charleston, SC
19 December 2010